To MAM

With love from

Russell & Val

x x

Growing Up in Kilvert Country

Growing Up in Kilvert Country

(Recollections of a Radnorshire Childhood)

Mona M. Morgan

First impression - 1990

ISBN 0 86383 680 1

This volume is published with the support of the Welsh Arts Council.

Printed by J. D. Lewis & Sons Ltd., Gomer Press, Llandysul, Dyfed.

Dedicated to my sister and brother
and to many friends of childhood
and adolescence

Contents

Author's Note

As the events here recorded happened some sixty or more years ago, I cannot guarantee that my memory is fault-free. Others may recall some things differently. I can only record things as I remember them and hope I may be forgiven for any errors.

To facilitate the telling of the story, events have sometimes been linked together and conversations and statements not always recorded where they actually happened. Nevertheless they are as true a record as my memory can provide of things that did actually happen and of words that were actually spoken. A glossary of dialect and unfamiliar words and phrases is included at the end of the book.

My thanks are due to my husband who offered valuable suggestions and checked the manuscript.

Introduction

My native county, formerly Radnorshire, now part of the huge county of Powys, was a county of hill and moorland, topped by crisp green turf, bracken, gorse, heather and whimberry, two-thirds being classified as mountain land. In Howitt's words it had

> *. . . wastes of heath*
> *Stretching for miles to lure the bee,*
> *Where the wild bird, on pinions strong,*
> *Wheels round, and pours his piping song,*
> *And timid creatures wander free.*

This hilly country of hidden waterfalls, rushing brooks and clear, lively streams, was, during my childhood, a remote, romantic place, undisturbed by the changes taking place in other parts of Britain. Its domestic routine and farming methods lagged several decades behind those of southern England, while its truly pastoral landscape was unmarred by industry of any kind, its bracing air pure and unpolluted.

Its unspoiled beauty captivated Byron, Shelley and the Wordsworth family, who were frequent visitors. Dorothy spent several short breaks at my birthplace, a small farmstead called Gwerndyfnant near Gladestry, at that time belonging to the Hutchinson's of Hindwell, her kinsfolk.

Radnorshire was a little-known county right up to the outbreak of the Second World War: even folks in distant parts of the neighbouring county of Hereford had never heard of the place. It had by far the sparsest population, per square mile, of any county in England and Wales. The bulk of the people was concentrated in the three small market towns of Presteigne, Knighton and Rhayader, situated along its borders, and in its spa and administrative centre, Llandrindod Wells, leaving the whole central area signally thinly peopled.

The county's largest river, the far-famed Wye, formed its boundary for many miles with the neighbouring county of Brecon: its lesser river valleys were hardly less picturesque.

Though most places bore Welsh names, or Welsh names that had been Anglicised, little or no Welsh was spoken except, perhaps, in the extreme north-west, bordering Montgomeryshire. Traces of the Welsh language were, however, still to be found in the local dialect and in the construction

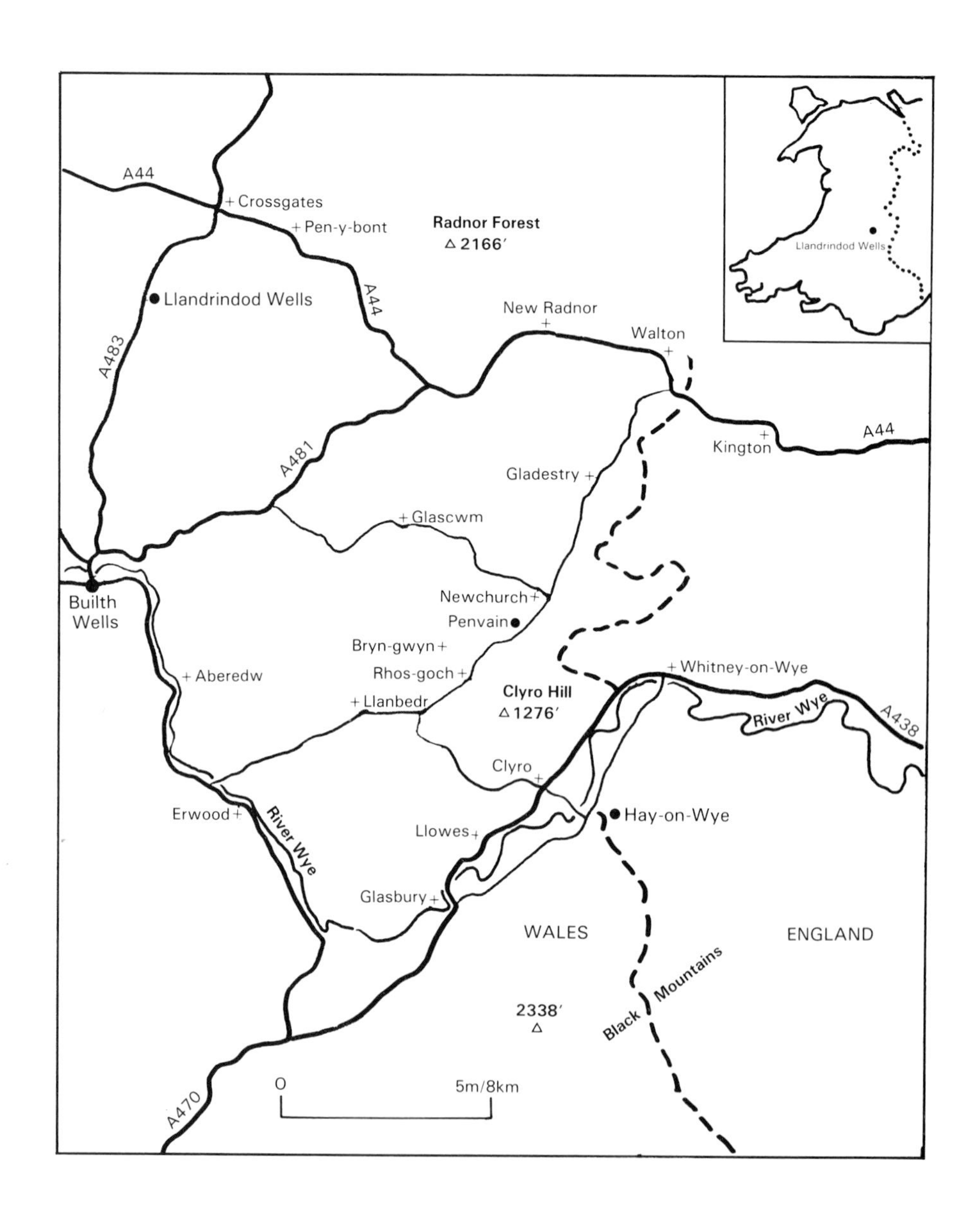

A44
Crossgates
Pen-y-bont
Radnor Forest
2166′
Llandrindod Wells
A44
A483
New Radnor
Walton
A481
Kington
A44
Gladestry
Glascwm
Builth Wells
Newchurch
Penvain
Bryn-gwyn
Rhos-goch
Aberedw
Whitney-on-Wye
Clyro Hill
1276′
Llanbedr
River Wye
A438
Clyro
Hay-on-Wye
Erwood
River Wye
Llowes
Glasbury
WALES
ENGLAND
Black Mountains
2338′
0
5m/8km
A470
Llandrindod Wells

of dialect phrases. The native speech had that lilting intonation characteristic of Welsh people.

The publication, in 1938, of Kilvert's Diary put Radnorshire, at last, firmly on the map. During the war years and the years of austerity following, the Diary became a favourite bed-side book of many a city-bound, war-weary soul, the peaceful scenes and events depicted in its pages soothing many a troubled breast.

Over the years the southeast portion of the county came to be known as 'The Radnorshire Kilvert Country' and is now a place of literary pilgrimage.

1. Earliest Memories

The Great War had been raging for exactly two years when I was born on the fourth of August, 1916, at a farm called Gwerndyfnant in the parish of Gladestry. It was an attractive residence, I am told, surrounded by rhododendrons and other shrubs, though since we moved to a farm called The Drewern in the neighbouring parish of Glascwm when I was still a babe-in-arms I have no recollection of it. I was the youngest of three children. My sister Muriel (known always as Mu) was seventeen months my senior, and my brother Arthur was five years old.

My earliest memory is of one fateful Monday at The Drewern when our parents had gone to Builth Wells market, leaving us in the charge of our grandmother. Arthur, then about ten years old, had taken a sickle and was cutting nettles in a field near the house. Mu and I skipped round him in our play. Suddenly Mu danced into the path of the sickle and screamed as the sharp blade bit deep into the calf of her leg. Panic-stricken, Arthur rushed to the house for Granny, who arrived to find a deep gash bleeding profusely. Today such a gash would merit immediate medical attention, but in those days there were no telephones in country districts and summoning a doctor meant saddling a horse and galloping to the nearest surgery. There was no one at hand that day to fetch a doctor, even if it had been deemed necessary, so Granny had to deal with the emergency as best she could, by bandaging the wound with strips of boiled calico smeared with Zambuc.

Upon our parents' return the blood-saturated bandage was soaked with warm water to free it, and the wound inspected, but it was not considered serious enough to warrant a medical opinion. Doctors were called only in gravest emergencies, for, apart from the botheration of summoning them, they had to be paid, and money was scarce. As a consequence Mu still carries a wide scar on her leg to remind us of this childhood incident.

In 1922, tragedy struck the family when our brother Arthur died of rheumatic fever. His death stunned the whole neighbourhood. Everyone said he had caught this fever through playing in the brook on his way to school and sitting all day with wet feet. Parents warned their children to keep out of the water and remember what had happened to little Arthur.

I well remember being taken to Arthur's bedroom to say goodbye to him, and being told that he was going away to live with Jesus. Though perplexed, I sensed the extreme solemnity of the occasion from the sad tone of Mother's voice and the tears that welled up in her eyes. Arthur appeared to be asleep but I knew instinctively that I would never see him again, and when Mother lifted me up to kiss his brow I was shocked to find it as cold as marble.

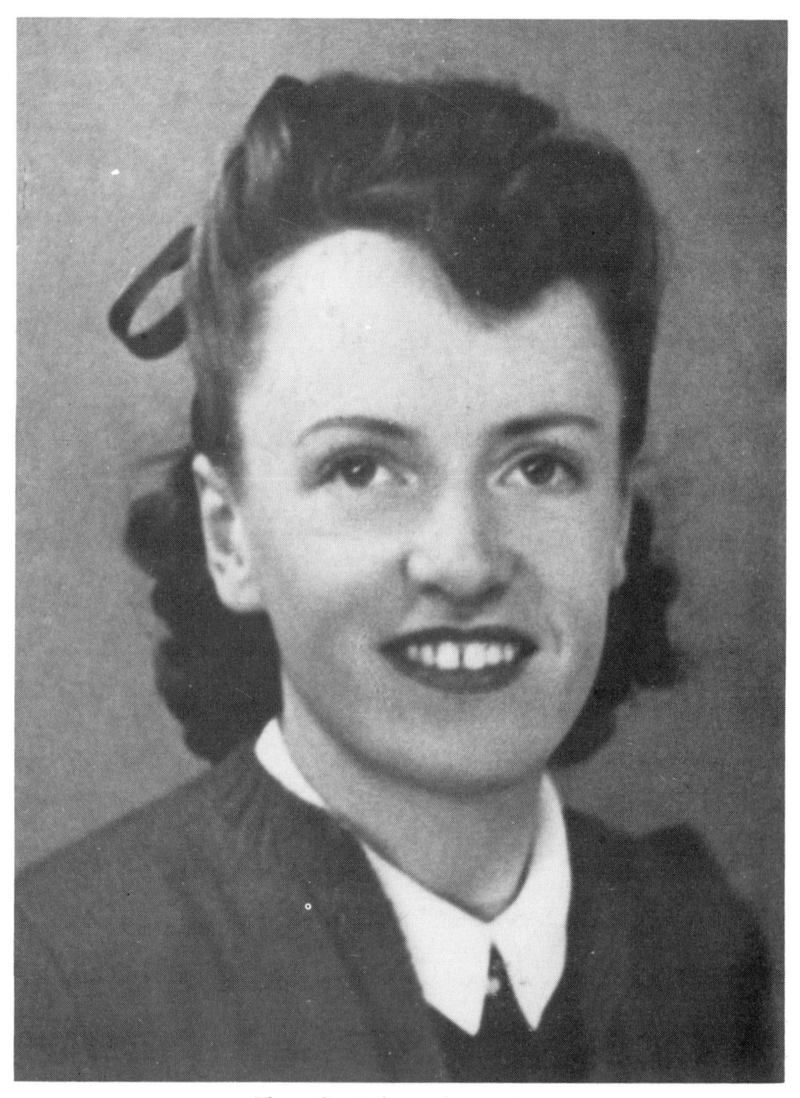

The author in her early twenties.

Mu in her late twenties.

I dimly remember the funeral with an unaccustomed crowd of people arriving for a service at the house. I recall walking with Mother the two miles or more to Franksbridge in procession behind the coffin, pausing at intervals for a change of bearers. A long procession of mourners followed us, all dressed entirely in black. As was the custom, the bearers had been provided with black gloves and armbands. Later, bereavement cards, in black-edged envelopes, were sent to relatives and friends, to be kept in Arthur's memory.

I doubt whether I realized the purpose of that sad journey, or that the bearers were carrying my brother's body. In those days children were discouraged from asking questions and were told only what their parents considered suitable. I had accepted that, in some mysterious way, Arthur had gone to live with Jesus, and no more was said on the subject.

Shortly after Arthur's death, the family moved again. Our new home was in the neighbouring parish of Newchurch, a remote place on the English border.

This move allowed Dad to own his farm for the first time, and his mind was full of ideas that he was itching to put into practice as soon as circumstances permitted. Of a single-minded, go-ahead character, he never allowed the grass to grow under his feet. He enjoyed intelligent conversation and a good joke, but was basically a serious person who never wasted words. Throughout his long life his advice was often sought and found to be pretty reliable. He was fortunate in having a wife who was always willing to fall in with his plans, ready at all times to help in any way she could. Mother was a lively, merry person, always chattering, an unassuming person who never put on airs, and whether in the company of rich or poor, sophisticated or naïve, was always herself.

Our grandmother had been a widow for several years. Although I was twelve years old when she died, at the age of eighty-two, my mental picture of her is strangely blurred. From information gathered over the years, it seems she had had a hard life bringing up her family on a small farm with insufficient support from a husband who apparently dissipated money and time that could have been put to better use.

In those motorless days country districts boasted no removal vans. People moved their few belongings on farm wagons, assisted by neighbours. The shortest possible route was taken, often via cart tracks over fields and hills, thereby almost halving the distance.

On the day we moved from The Drewern, Mother wakened us early. The men were waiting to dismantle our bedstead for the journey. The rest of the bedroom furniture had been carried downstairs the previous evening, so we awoke to a bare and hollow-sounding room. Downstairs all was hugger-mugger, with carts and items of furniture scattered about waiting to be loaded. As we ate our makeshift breakfast men bustled in and out, puffing and grunting as they humped heavy articles towards the door.

When all the wagons had been piled high and were ready for the journey, the family climbed into the pony trap and set off along the cart track through the pasture above the house. After passing a tumble-down cottage known as Duppas we were soon on the open hill. The journey promised to be a bumpy one, with the trap swaying from side to side on its springs as its wheels slipped in and out of the ruts. The track wound steadily over the crest of the hill before gradually sloping down to where four tracks converged, near a large green mound called The Giant's Grave. What pictures that green mound conjured up in our childish imaginations! From there we turned left, to follow a well-defined track that hugged the fence at the foot of the hill, here and there fording a stream. At intervals someone had to alight to open and close the gates that barred our way. Eventually we reached the steep gradient overlooking the village of Glascwm in its deep green vale. Here our rough ride ended as we joined the main road. To relieve the strain on the pony the grown-ups alighted for the stiff climb up Rhiw Fwnws, just beyond the village, resuming their seats at the summit.

For us children the day was an adventure. Until now we had trodden only familiar paths; today each fold in the hills revealed a new vista, and by the time we reached Newchurch village so many unfamiliar scenes had been unfolded that our erstwhile haunts seemed worlds away. We felt a certain sadness in leaving behind all that was familiar and, despite the excitement of seeing so much that was new, felt a slight apprehension of the unknown, especially the prospect of starting our new school, which Dad had pointed out to us *en route*, standing isolated beside the road, a mile or more from Newchurch village.

We found our new farm off the Newchurch—Rhos-goch road, half a mile beyond the village. It was approached by a rough, stony lane with high banks on one side and a babbling stream on the other. By a large pool we turned left, through the fold gate, the lane itself continuing straight ahead to Newchurch Hill.

The farmstead stood on a shelf of land overlooking the Milw valley and a hill known as The Little Mountain. From the wainhouse corner we caught first sight of our new home. It was a long, rambling, stone-built house with little pretension to beauty. Originally it had been a low building with one large dormer window in the centre of the roof, but some years prior to our arrival a two-storey, gabled extension had been added at either end. Each of the two extensions had one large downstairs room, with two bedrooms overhead. The bedrooms in the centre section had fallen into disuse and become attics.

While we awaited the arrival of the furniture, Dad showed us over the house. We entered by the back door and came into a large flag-stoned kitchen which extended the width of the house. This room was, in fact, to become the heart of the house, where the family would work, eat and relax before the fire on winter evenings. The room had two windows, one overlooking the fold and The Little Mountain, the other facing the distant garden, the old house (relic of an earlier age), and gorse-covered banks and fields stretching up to Newchurch Hill. Deep in the wall on the right of the kitchen range was the baking oven, and on the left a deep recess which the grown-ups decided would neatly accommodate our large mahogany-coloured cupboard.

While the adults discussed the positioning of the main items of furniture, we gazed through the windows, hardly able to credit that we would be living amongst these strange surrounding. What places to explore!

We followed Dad up two stone steps to the passage door, alongside which a second door gave access to the stairs leading to the two bedrooms overhead. One of these was to be for Arnold, the waggoner, who, with other helpers, was on his way with the household effects and farm equipment. The adjoining bedroom would be reserved for any extra farm servant that might subsequently be hired. The passage, like the kitchen, was stone-flagged, and on its right, facing the front door, we found the cold, north-facing pantry with its salting-stone and deep-set window half-covered with perforated zinc to let in the fresh air and keep out the flies.

Next we came to a large square room which was to be the sitting room. This room, as it turned out, would be seldom used, for the family were to find little time for lounging. On the far side of this room was yet another passage, with three doors opening off it. One led to the dairy, where the churn and butter-making equipment were housed. The second, at the far end of the passage, opened into a very pleasant room which, like the kitchen, extended the width of the house. This was the only room with a boarded floor. It had a large sash window on either side of the chimney breast and an outside door. Because it was so far from the kitchen, it was impracticable as a living room and eventually became the granary. Through the third door we found a small hall, from where another flight of stairs led to bedrooms and attics. The larger of the two bedrooms, we were to share with Granny. The other, which had a fire-grate, was to be for Mother and Dad.

On completion of the tour, Mother and Granny, not surprisingly, described the house as 'very inconvenient'. Dad agreed, but reminded them that a farmer's chief concern when viewing a farm was to ensure that the land was fertile—the house was of secondary importance. However, he promised that he had in mind a scheme for improvements, and after a few years these were indeed carried out. Three new bedrooms were constructed in the centre section to replace the attics, and a staircase to serve them built opposite the front door. The dairy was incorporated into the pantry, so that all rooms in daily use were much more conveniently situated. At the same time a small area in front of the house was enclosed within wooden railings for a flower garden, with gated paths leading to the front and back doors.

Immediately Arnold arrived, Mu and I rushed him off to see his bedroom and then took him to see ours. When he saw how far away from the kitchen our bedroom was, he teased us by saying that he would be snugly tucked up in his bed long before we had even reached ours.

Behind the house was a high bank, crowned by a large sycamore tree, whilst a gorse-covered mound overlooked the old house. Between these two banks a stream trickled down to form a pond. The overflow was piped under a path that led from the back door, down past the old house to the garden. There, screened behind bushes, just inside the gate, was the privy. Beside the garden another gorsy bank had at its foot a deep well of ice-cold water. The well's overflow joined that from the pond and together they formed a second, larger pond, under twin elms, near the fold gate. The ground had been raised at the lower end of this pond to increase its depth and area and to form a cart track leading from the fold to the fields.

Several fields on the farm still carried their old Welsh names. There was Cae Milw—the field through which the Milw brook ran; Cae Blaidd—the wolf's pasture; Cae Drain—the thorn field; Dol-garn—the rocky pasture; and two fields called The Panneys (Pannau)—the fields of hollows. The rest had lost their Welsh names and become The Poolpiece, The Far Meadow, and so on.

Our parish of Newchurch was one of the few Welsh parishes in the neighbourhood to have an English name. Nearby parishes, on the Welsh side of the border, still had their descriptive Welsh names. There was Rhos-goch—the red moor; Bryn-gwyn—the white hill; Glascwm—the green valley; and Colfa—a gap in the hills.

Newchurch parish boasted no manor house or stately home but was made up chiefly of small farms and smallholdings. All parishioners enjoyed more or less the same status; all were bound by common tasks and shared a common leisure. The close-knit, mainly self-sufficient community shared each other's joys and sorrows, ready with a listening ear and helping hand.

As is common in Wales, many families bore the same surnames and were distinguished by the names of their dwellings (John the Wern, Bill the Mill, and so on). Some less intelligent mortals, regularly addressed in this way, remained quite ignorant of their surnames and were highly amused when someone addressed them correctly.

Our new farm was called Penvain, a name that had over the years been corrupted from the pure Welsh. Its correct name was probably Penwaun, meaning 'at the top of the meadow or moor', for that was where it had its location. The neighbouring farms, which we were to come to know almost as well as our own, bore their original Welsh names. These included Ty'n-y-cwm—the house in the dingle; Dolbedwen—the birch meadow; and Gilfach-yr-heol—the sheltered nook by the roadside.

2. The Farm

The farm, of some ninety-odd acres, was mixed arable and pasture, with two permanent meadows. It carried a small herd of milking cows and their calves, a team of cart horses, a pony and a couple of pigs. But, like all upland farms, Penvain was primarily a sheep farm, with the right to turn so many sheep, according to its acreage, on to the adjoining hills. These hill flocks were permanent ones, knowing their own boundaries and rarely straying far beyond them. Ewe lambs were kept with the flock and older ewes sold to make room for them. The lambs grew up with their mothers and automatically stayed within bounds. Sheep from neighbouring farms regularly overlapped on the common boundary, but when a dog was sent to round them up each flock automatically ran to its own side.

Apart from the waggoner, who lived in, and a workman who came daily from a nearby cottage, only casual labourers were employed. These were mainly roadsters, who tramped the country seeking work between drinking sprees. Permanently thirsty, they chose employment on farms where they could depend on a plentiful supply of cider. They slept in the barn and had their meals served there. Several of these men were

The wagonner and his team.

employed at Penvain, though I can clearly recall but two. One, a big man with a long rolling gait, who always wore yorks around his trousers, was known as Big George. The other, known throughout the district as Radnor Tom, spent much of his time at Penvain. Whatever job he was given to do was done conscientiously, though he always maintained that he could have done it better had he been provided with the correct tools. 'Well, you canna do a tidy job if you hanna got the proper tools,' was his invariable complaint.

Radnor Tom, always clean in his person, was eventually promoted to having his meals in the kitchen, on a small table beside the sink. He ate with more gusto than grace, smacking his lips appreciatively, especially when served with his favourite spring onions and cheese. He used his table-knife as he had previously used a clasp-knife, to convey his food to his mouth, and habitually licked the neck of his sauce-bottle after use! In time a cancerous sore broke out on his lower lip, and we lost sight of him for a time. Eventually he returned with a scar. All went well for a time, till the sore returned and spread. He left one day never to return.

In summer, at the edge of night, the roadsters could be seen making their way to the barn, to climb the ladder to their beds in the fragrant hay, carrying in one hand a pail to serve as a chamber-pot. Clothes worn throughout the day served as nightwear. A change of underwear was carried in a small bundle on a stick over the shoulder. Their laundry was done in their spare time and hung to dry in their sleeping-quarters. When they left, a strong smell of corduroy, twist-tobacco and cider permeated the barn for days.

In those days of little mechanization farming was a laborious life. Soil on upland farms needed much manure and hard labour to produce worthwhile crops. There were no government grants or subsidies: every man was on his own, his success depending on strenuous effort and good husbandry. Even then, if disease struck his livestock or storms or drought ruined his crops, disaster stared him in the face. Nevertheless, given reasonable luck it was a rewarding job which allowed a man to see the result of his labour; an occupation in which a job well done brought immense fulfilment; an unhurried occupation in which men took no account of the hours put in.

* * * *

By today's standards farmhouse work was drudgery, with no labour-saving devices of any kind to relieve the back-breaking toil. No maid-servant was kept at Penvain and most of the work fell on Mother. Granny, of course, did her fair share while she was able, but folks were considered old at seventy then, their working lives over. It was at this stage of her life that I best remember Granny, sitting beside the fire, a shawl over her shoulders and a black, lacy widow's cap threaded with mauve ribbon on her head. Granny still had a smattering of Welsh in her vocabulary, using such words as *cwt* (sty); *gwern* (swamp); *pwn*[*io*] (to beat); *cornel* (corner); *dowlod (taflod)* (loft); [*c*]*whirligwgan* (spinning-top); *gwdihŵ* (owl). When we were stuck for a game Granny would suggest, 'Why not play ball for a hurry?' (short time) or 'Why not take a walk up the fields albease?' (leisurely).

Mother, a light-hearted person, usually saw the funny side when things went wrong. 'Well, isn't that enought to sicken a snipe?' she'd enquire, before dissolving into laughter, adding for the benefit of any surprised bystanders, 'Well, might as well laugh, for crying will do no good.' When she was undecided on what course to take, a favourite expression was, 'Well, I don't know whether to bake or buy bread.'

A small, trim person, Mother was nimble and quick, getting through an enormous amount of work in a short time. Full of vitality, she was the first to rise each morning, tripping quickly down the stairs well before 6 a.m. to busy herself in clearing the flues, rising the ashes and lighting the fire with the morning wood that had dried overnight on the hob.

When breakfast was over and our school lunch satchels packed, she donned an old gaberdine raincoat and felt hat and made her way to the beast-house with the milking pails. There, seated on her three-legged stool, she pressed her head against a cow's flank, pulling and squeezing the teats to squirt milk, with a thin, rasping sound, into the pail wedged between her knees. As one cow was stripped she moved to the next. Occasionally her raised voice could be heard scolding a restless cow as it slashed her face with its tail or kicked and threatened to upset the bucket. Some cows had calves to rear, and as she milked on one side the calf sucked on the other, snatching the teats from her hands as it butted the udder. We always knew when the job was nearing completion because the sound of the milk filling the pail changed to a soft roar.

The milk was strained through butter-muslin into large pans and left for the cream to rise to the surface to be skimmed off into enamel pails for butter-making. Many farms had leads—square, concave tables lined with lead, each with a brass stopper in the centre for releasing the milk. With the arrival of the separator, leads were discarded and the milk strained into the separator's large metal bowl. As Mother took its handle to commence separating she invariably broke into song with one of her favourite hymns. After use the separator had to be dismantled; the many steel cups, which fitted into each other, had to be separated and washed individually before all the parts were scalded and reassembled.

Now time could be given to the poultry, for it was from poultry, butter and eggs that Mother derived her income. Feeding, collecting the eggs, cleaning the fowl-houses, and occasionally creosoting them against red-mite, took up a large slice of Mother's day.

There was no water laid on in the farmhouse: all had to be carried from the well some five hundred yards from the house. The water was heated in large, heavy cast-iron kettles and in a fountain, all suspended from the pivoted sway over the fire, or in the boiler of the range. Kettle-holders were essential for grasping the hot handles.

During the morning the fire was allowed to die down for the grate to be black-leaded. For this and all dirty jobs such as brushing accumulated soot from kettles, pots and pans and cleaning the fender and fire-irons with Brasso and brickdust, Mother, over her ordinary apron, wore a coarse apron made of sacking. Before being swept and scrubbed, the flagstones were sprinkled with damp tea-leaves to help lay the dust.

All beds were filled with goose feathers stripped from their quills. Bed-making was a time-consuming job, for all beds had to be stripped and pummelled before being made up. All this agitation created fluff and dust, necessitating daily mopping and dusting.

Large meals had to be prepared for men coming in with appetites healthy from open-air work. For dinner the meat most commonly served was bacon. If a hen refused to lay or met with an accident, we had boiled fowl for a change. Roast or stewed rabbit made a cheap and appetising meal which helped to vary the diet. I enjoyed the rabbit's head, cracking the skull to find the delicious brains. Fish was never found on the menu, except for the rare gift of salmon brought by some kind poacher.

A favourite pudding was roly-poly made with currants (Spotted Dick) or jam. The pudding was rolled in a greased pudding-cloth tied at each end like a sausage and boiled in the pot with the meat and vegetables. When plenty of fresh fruit was available a fruit suet pudding was made in a basin covered with a greased pudding-cloth and, again, boiled with the meat. Fruit tart and custard, or tapioca, rice or sago pudding, were usually served with roast or stewed meat.

When the table had been laid, one of us children was dispatched to the cellar with a quart jug to draw cider for the men. On fine days we skipped along the path at the foot of the bank behind the house to reach the outside cellar steps; in wet weather we went through the house to the indoor steps leading down from the far passage. The cider barrels, arranged on a low platform at one end, shared the cellar with a large heap of potatoes whose long, etiolated shoots strained upward, in springtime, towards the small window at the top of the wall. The place reeked of cider, damp earth and potatoes.

At tea-time a loaf of bread was placed on the bread-board for all adults to cut their own bread-and-butter, bread-and-jam or bread-and-cheese; they also cut their own wedge of cake or tart.

Washing, baking and churning days were extra busy. Rarely was Mother able to snatch a couple of hours of an afternoon to sit down to sew. How she enjoyed these quiet afternoons spent in making our dresses, petticoats and nighties, and Dad's flannel shirts, with just the tick of the kitchen clock for company. She also patched and mended torn garments and turned sheets side-to-middle to prolong their lives. On the odd occasion when nothing urgent awaited her attention she made patchwork quilts, crocheted gloves and made rag rugs for the hearth from worn garments, and clothes for our dolls.

3. Childhood's Unheeded Dream

There was little resemblance between my sister and me, either in looks or personality. Mu, pale-complexioned and brown-eyed, had long chestnut hair. I had the pink-and-white complexion that blushed readily, causing me intense embarrassment. My short, fine, blonde hair was worn in a fringe above my blue-grey eyes.

Mu was a tomboy, up to all kinds of antics, never happier than when entertaining friends with tom-foolery or leading us into some mischievous escapade. Normally quiet and placid, I had a fiery temper when roused. I, too, enjoyed the company of friends but was content occasionally to play alone. For most of the time we played harmoniously, Mu making most of the decisions but every so often I disagreed with her and quarrels broke out, causing Mother to chide us for being 'spleenish with each other'. Then there were the odd days when we repeatedly got into mischief and Mother declared we were 'burning in our skins'. These escapades usually ended with a stinging slap across our bare legs.

The world of our early childhood was a silent one. The still, small voices of nature could still be heard; the tinkling of rills, the churring of grasshoppers and the language and progress of small creatures about their daily pursuits. In the fall of the year, when bird-song had ceased and small creatures had crept away to hibernate, the silence could be eerie, frightening one into imagining that all life had perished, that one was alone in a silent, empty world.

The only unnatural sounds that disturbed the quiet were the whirr of the mower in summer, the rumble and clank of the reaper at harvest and the drone of the threshing machine in autumn; noises neither harsh nor strident, but compatible with the countryside.

In an environment brim-full of new things to discover and wonder at, our days were busy and absorbing. In retrospect we see them as enchanting days, care-free and blissful, when cuckoos called from early dawn to setting sun. All childish worries and frustrations that fretted and vexed have been veiled, leaving only highlights of happiness to shine through.

Ours was a stable world in which things had changed little for centuries. Where centuries-old farms and cottages, mellowed with age, merged into the landscape; where people spent a lifetime in the same parish. It was an easy-going, affable world, where everyone knew everyone else; a world in which people accepted limitations and learned to be content; a leisurely world not ruled by the clock; a world in which folks still found time to 'stand and stare'.

We were hemmed about by friendship, love and security, with a loving Mother always at hand to listen, console and advise. We felt wanted and important, big fish in a small pond. Nevertheless, discipline was strict; moral values were upheld. We were brought up to be dutiful and obedient, to be trustworthy and honest, to respect our elders and show courtesy to others. We were left in no doubt as to what we should or should not do. When parents said 'No' there was no argument. Disobedience was firmly nipped in the bud; any suggestion of defiance or insolence instantly reprimanded. Parents turning a blind eye to any of these things were said to be 'making a rod for their own backs'. In common with all our contemporaries we resented this discipline, but almost without exception respected the disciplinarians and had little deference for those we could disobey with impunity.

Living in a community where everyone knew everyone else tended to make us guard our characters and shrink from doing anything we'd be ashamed for others to hear about. This, no doubt, was and still is a powerful deterrent against crime in the countryside.

Urged by parents and teachers to make the most of our time and talents, we were reminded that 'time is fleeting' and that 'the mill can never grind with the water that has passed'. We were not allowed to forget that

To each is given a book of rules,
An hour-glass and a set of tools.
And each must build ere life has flown
A stumbling-block or a stepping stone.

Everything worthwhile in life, we were told, had to be earned; 'easy winning made the prize light'.

Hymns and verses sought to teach moral values and self-discipline:

Yield not to temptation, for yielding is sin;
Each victory will help you some other to win.
Fight manfully onward, dark passions subdue,
Look ever to Jesus, He will carry you through.

Shun evil companions, bad language disdain,
God's name hold in reverence, nor take it in vain.
Be thoughtful and earnest, kind-hearted and true,
Look ever to Jesus, He will carry you through.

Much of this advice, no doubt, fell on deaf ears; none of us grew up to be a saint but there is little doubt that these ethics, regularly instilled into impressionable minds, influenced our future beliefs and moulded our characters. As an old minister was fond of saying, 'People with a sound, Christian upbringing may occasionally slip on deck, but they rarely fall overboard'.

Whatever else may be said for these methods, at least they seemed to work. No child that I knew grew up with a police record: violence and crime was practically non-existent and still had the power to shock and horrify.

Dad was our family disciplinarian and when he was around we had to mind our p's and q's. Up on the bacon cratch he kept a small cane which he dubbed 'the plant'. If he had cause to speak more than once, a quick glance up at the cratch, with the enquiry, 'Where's that plant?' brought the desired effect: there was never any need to bring it down.

Dad was a perfectionist, believing that if a job was worth doing it was worth doing well. Rather inclined to impatience he was not the man to suffer fools gladly. We soon learned that it paid to give his every instruction our undivided attention. Both my sister and I have grown up to give careful attention to detail, whether as a result of our upbringing, bearing out the truth of the old maxim that 'as the twig is bent, so the tree will grow', or because we are just 'chips off the old block'. Who can say?

As young children we had few toys and made our own fun. In suitable weather, throughout the year, much of our time was spent in our play-house, high up on the gorse-covered mound behind the old house. The clear area on the top, reached by a narrow path through the prickly bushes, made a fine large kitchen and a couple of smaller areas, opening off it, served as additional rooms. With broken crockery, old kettles, pots and pans purloined from the rubbish heap, we bustled around, tirelessly performing our household tasks. With these make-shift things we were far happier than many children showered with expensive toys, easily come by and lightly valued. Our spontaneous, make-believe play thoroughly absorbed and satisfied us.

From our high vantage point we were able to see and hear all that went on around us. We paused in our play to watch the lambs running races up and down the banks of the Gorsty Field. We heard the pheasant's mating call in Llanoley Wood; our old Herefordshire rabbit-catcher heard this too, announcing at the dinner-table, 'There's a pheasant in the wood, Boss, I 'eard 'im say "cock-up" and shek 'is feamers.' In May we laughed to see the cows, released from their winter quarters, galloping wildly round the Poolpiece with outstretched tails and tossing horns, kicking and prancing like ungainly lambs in their joy to be free.

In June an overgreedy bullock, with swollen body and poker-stiff legs, lay dead in the new rich grass in the cloverfield. We stood for some time in the presence of death, wondering, wondering.

In summer's heat, panic-stricken cows galloped, with outstretched tails and staring eyes, round and round the Poolpiece in an effort to escape the gadfly. 'Oh, look, the cows are on the bree,' we told each other.

Occasionally, on a fine day in late autumn, we caught the sound of the huntsman's horn or his 'view halloo' as a fox was sighted. Or perhaps it was the sound of the pack giving tongue as they picked up the scent that reached our ears before we spotted them fanning out over a distant slope, followed by the riders. One day a close-up yelp surprised us, and there, at the foot of our mound, were red-coated huntsmen on well-groomed horses, followed by black-coated riders, with a motley crowd on mounts of all shapes and sizes bringing up the rear. We watched entranced till they disappeared from view, then broke into the song we had learned at school:

Oh the yelping of hounds, the skelping
Along the covert and out at the back.
Oh the galloping, Oh the walloping,
Oh the rush of the gone-away Jack.
Off like a feather he floats on the heather,
Blackberry calling the tune in his track.
One more double, across the stubble, and he's in trouble
And tossed by the pack.

Each week our play was interrupted to watch the corn-merchant's team of horses labouring up the lane with the old covered wagon, bringing corn and meal for the animals. On rare occasions the man with the entire horse was to be seen coming up the lane, the great mettlesome beast prancing by his side. Sometimes we met them on the road, the apparently irascible beast still prancing and taking up so much of the road that we were forced to cower in the ditch till they had passed.

Barking dogs or cackling geese alerted us to the arrival of visitors. The geese on the lower pool were first-class sentinels, giving us timely warning of anyone approaching. They drew our attention to the arrival of a tramp in ragged, ill-fitting clothes and broken boots, clutching in his grimy hand the wire handle of his tea-tin. There was nothing unusual in the sight of a tramp, for we often met one on the road. Some were ill-tempered and we carefully turned our eyes away lest we should annoy them by staring.

With Mother present we had no such fear and raced down to the back door for a closer look at this particular one. We were just in time to see him hand his tea-tin over for Mother to fill with scalding tea. His skin, grimed with dirt, was probably washed only by rain and dew and wiped with his coat sleeve. His long, matted hair stuck out in whisps from his battered hat. His broken shoes revealed filthy feet. Afterwards we felt sorry for his wretched plight but Mother accused him of indolence, saying that he could find work to support himself if he tried.

When a swarthy gipsyman begged leave to pull his caravan into a field for a night or two, permission was given reluctantly, for often when gipsies left something went with them. Though we feared gipsies, we were fascinated by them and loved to pass near their encampment, in the company of an adult, to see the women stirring their pots, suspended from tripods over a wood fire, while their men-folk sat making pegs with wood purloined from nearby hedges. The children lounged around the caravan with whippet dogs or sat on the steps while the old, scraggy, piebald horse made the most of his opportunity by browsing. Nothing would persuade us to pass the encampment alone: we feared the power of these clairvoyant, crystal-gazing folk, suspecting them of sorcery and bewitchment.

When cackling geese heralded the arrival of a gipsy woman with a large basket on her arm, followed by a couple of ragged children, we scampered down from the playhouse for a closer look. We were intrigued by the gipsy's swarthy, weather-beaten skin, her greasy, plaited hair and her large ear-rings. She called Mother a pretty lady, assuring her that her lucky face would one day bring her good fortune, and offered to predict her future if Mother would cross her palm with silver. Her basket contained clothes-pegs, papers of pins, knots of tape, combs, ribbons and laces. She begged for food and clothing, painting, the while, a distressing picture of the life and lot of the gipsy. We listened, spell-bound, to every word she uttered.

When, from time to time, Mu was called upon to help Mother, I hurried to the old house where the dark blue winnowing machine was kept. A raised panel on one side of it made a capital blackboard on which to write sums and spellings for my doll and other imaginary pupils. From the ceiling, dust-laden cobwebs moved in the breeze; hens popped in for their dust-baths in the powdery earth floor. In the old chimney-corner the ducks had their smelly nests; dusty planks and other eyesores leaned against the walls. Quite oblivious to these sordid surroundings, I pictured myself, immaculately dressed, standing before my class of pupils in a neat classroom. What immense satisfaction I derived from writing sums and spellings on my blackboard, teaching, demonstrating and correcting. At that time my favourite book was *The Woodrow Book*—a book of nature stories—which I repeatedly pestered someone to read to me. In time I knew the whole book by heart and read it to my pupils, following the words as I did so. What joy was mine, one day, to find I could actually read!

My 'class readers' were leaflets taken from 'Doan's Backache Kidney Pill' cartons. These I distributed amongst my pupils and, with no one to criticize, pronounced the words in my own way. The word 'system' cropped up frequently and this, I assured my pupils, was pronounced 'sigh-stem'. Though the pupils were little the wiser at the end of the lesson, the teacher, through trial and error, benefitted considerably.

Occasionally the classroom was transformed into a concert hall and, standing on a block of wood, I recited poem after poem to the imaginary audience, now and then favouring them with a solo. At first they had to be content with simple poems:

My Shadow

I have a little shadow that goes in and out with me,
But what can be the use of him is more than I can see.
He is very, very like me from my heels up to my head,
And I see him jump before me when I jump into my bed.

The funniest thing about him is the way he likes to grow,
Not at all like proper children, which is often very slow.
He sometimes shoots up taller like an india-rubber ball,
And he sometimes gets so little that there's none of him at all.

One morning, very early, before the sun was up,
I rose and found the shining dew on every buttercup.
But my lazy little shadow, like an arrant sleepy-head,
Had stayed at home behind me and was fast asleep in bed.

As I grew older and the poems learned became slightly more exacting, I put heart and soul into my renderings, trying to enunciate clearly as I had been taught. I tried to put emphasis where I thought it was called for; I used my lips to labialize the consonants and tried to make sure that words ending with consonants were clearly separated from those commencing with vowels. In my own opinion I outclassed all *eisteddfod* competitors I had ever heard, but would doubtless have suffered a painful humiliation had I been put to the test. When reciting before a live audience, I was far too shy to put into effect all I had practised, for my blushing cheeks caused me intense embarrassment and my only thought was to get it over and get back to my seat.

With a flair for learning verse I knew all the other children's poems, as well as my own, by the time the concert or anniversary arrived. Over the years I committed dozens to memory, as well as psalms and passages of scripture, most of which I can clearly remember still. We were never enlightened as to the authors of the poems—they were apparently considered unimportant.

4. Springtime

The first warm sunny spring day found us impatient to wear lighter clothes, but were told that spring could be a treacherous time, its sunny days deceptive. After the rigours of winter everyone was at a low ebb and care was needed. The old folks said:

March will search, April try,
May will tell whether you'll live or die.

During the winter we had been treated with black-currant tea for colds, goosegrease on hot brown paper applied to tight chests, a spoonful of goose-oil for a raw throat (very relieving when one could overcome the thought of swallowing it), or fat bacon tied around the neck with a woollen sock (equally difficult to accept). Our cuts and abrasions were disinfected with stinging iodine and soothed with Zambuc or Germoline. Men's sprains and strains were rubbed with Sloan's Liniment or embrocation.

Now was the time for spring tonics. First came internal cleansing with senna tea. How we detested the stuff! There was Clarke's Blood-mixture to purify the blood. To build us up we were given brimstone and treacle, cod-liver oil and malt, Scott's Emulsion, Virol and Parish's Food, all, with the exception of Virol, thoroughly unpleasant to take.

In common with all outdoor activity on the farm our childhood pastimes were influenced, to a large extent, by the seasons. In springtime, when pastures were studded with daisies, larches veiled with green, and new life stirred in the woods, we bent our steps towards the copse by Ty'n-y-cwm's Stable Field to search for primroses and violets—primmeroses and vilets as we called them.

Our story-books painted enchanting pictures of copses on moonlit nights, when hidden doors in oak-trunks opened to reveal long halls, lit by countless lamps, leading to fairy abodes of unending bliss. Rings of fairies, with sparkling wands and gauzy wings, might be seen dancing in a clearing, dryads or other fabulous folk engaged in revelry. These unseen folk figured largely in our day-dreams and, though we never really expected to meet them, a copse, we secretly felt, was a likely place to come upon an elf on a toadstool or a ring of sparkling fairies in a glade. One poem we learned went some way to describing our copse:

There's a little wood with moss in it and beetles,
And a little stream that quietly runs through.

And you wouldn't think they'd dare to come merry-making there.
But they do.

The trees in our copse grew higgledy-piggledy, their trunks lichen covered. Here and there a fallen mossy trunk made a capital resting place. As we entered, quists, startled by our approach, burst from the trees with a clatter of wings, leaving a deepened stillness in their wake. The woodland ways, which in autumn had been dank and sad, smelling of damp moss and rotting leaves, now were sunny and cheerful with the smell of rising sap and bursting leaves. Everywhere were signs of new life. Pale green buds decked the hawthorn and pussy willows shone like patches of sunlight. The copse was starred with the delicate blooms of anemones, but these we ignored, knowing their limp stems would wilt in our hands, never to recover. Instead we searched for primroses in mossy banks and violets in shady dells.

We peered in hawthorn bushes for the mossy nest of the chaffinch and searched the bank for the robin's nest. The names of common birds, trees and flowers were never consciously learned: all were part of the country vocabulary. The mating of birds and animals, witnessed almost from babyhood, was innocently accepted as part of the natural scheme of things.

On a sunny morning we paid a spring visit to the shallow pond amongst the gorse bushes on Newchurch Hill, where masses of frog-spawn, like black-spotted tapioca pudding, lay in the clear water. Peewits swooped and twisted, repeatedly calling their own names. The haunting call of the curlew evoked pictures of windswept open spaces, as did the mournful mew of the buzzard. Here and there bright yellow gorse flowers shone in the sun, brightening an otherwise drab landscape. One or another gorse-bush was always in bloom, for it was said that when gorse is out of flower, kissing is out of fashion.

We broke off slippery chunks of jelly for our jam jars, adding a bit of pondweed to make a homely environment for the tadpoles when they hatched. On the sunny window-sill the black spots lengthened into tadpoles, which swam around in the water, opening and shutting their wee mouths as they came upon some tasty morsel too small for our eyes to see. As we replenished the jars with fresh pond water full of microscopic life the tadpoles grew and developed. 'Quick! Quick! They've got legs,' cried the first to make the discovery, as though, at any moment, they might disappear. With the arrival of the back legs we searched for suitable stones for the jars, to allow the tadpoles, which by now were developing lungs, to come to the surface to breathe. Gradually the tails shortened and eventually disappeared, leaving minute frogs which finally hopped out of the jars to begin a new life in the big world outside.

There were no perambulators in our part of the country in those days, so, like all mothers, we took our dolls for walks in shawls. One end of the shawl was wrapped around the doll and the other taken over the shoulder and under the other arm. A favourite walk was along the top of the Banky Field, from where we had a good view of the countryside. In early spring we saw the waggoner with his cartload of muck—the tail-board removed and the cart tipped—raking it out into heaps as the cart moved slowly forward. To us it looked an easy job but muck-carting was exhausting work, every soggy, heavy forkful having first to be thrown up into the cart from the mixen and later laboriously scattered—some twenty cartloads to the acre. Later we saw the fields being ploughed. Long before we were awake the waggoner had risen to feed, water and gear his team before breakfast, ready to turn out to plough at about 8.00 a.m. Ploughing, in those pre-tractor days, was a quiet occupation, and from the Banky Field we could hear the plod of the horses' feet, the jangle of the gears, the creak of the plough, and the ploughman's voice instructing his team. Behind him, flocks of screaming gulls swooped and dived for the worms turned out by the ploughshare. Seeing him reminded us of a song we learned at school:

Come all you jolly plough-boys and listen to me,
I'll sing in the praise of you all,
For if we don't labour how can we get bread,
Let's sing and be merry withal.

There's April, there's May, there is June and July,
What pleasure to see the corn grow;
In August we moil it, we reap, sheaf and tie,
And go down with our scythes for to mow.

Then when we have laboured and reaped every sheaf,
And gleanèd up every ear,
We'll make no more to do but to plough we will go,
To provide for the very next year.

Later, when all the muck had been ploughed in, we saw him harrowing with tooth-harrows to break up the clods. If he was preparing the field for roots he would plough and harrow it a second time, perhaps even a third, for root crops required a very fine tilth. Later still he was to be seen following the rattling Cambridge Roller, enveloped in a cloud of dust.

In a distant field, where corn had been sown, flocks of birds settled to feast on the grain, blatantly ignoring both the wooden, straw-padded meowkin in his old jacket and bowler hat, valiantly spreading his wooden arms to scare them, and the dead crows suspended from sticks to warn would-be thieves of their fate.

At some stage in our walks we came upon the hedger intertwining stems, half-cut through, between upright stakes. His equipment consisted of a beetle to hammer in the stakes, a sharp axe, a hacker and a pair of thick, clumsy hedging gloves. Nearby was a pile of newly cut stakes and a large bunch of hetherings to tie down and neaten the finished hedge. One spring in Dolgarn pastures, we met Jim the hedger, limping home, ashen-faced and sick, his boot oozing blood where the sharp axe had slipped and gashed his foot between the toes.

Once, when Mu was busy, I chose to take my doll along the high bank overlooking the gorse-filled lane, where I could search for birds' nests in the hedge. With all my concentration riveted on the hedge I caught my toe under an exposed gorse root and, with my arms fettered in the shawl, was catapulted headfirst down into the prickly bushes. How my temper flared as gorse needles pricked me all over! Lashing myself into a blind fury I extricated myself from the bushes, howling with rage and bristling all over with gorse. Furious with everyone and everything, I vented my spleen on the poor doll, shaking her mercilessly and calling the gorse bushes every evil name I knew, before running home to Mother for sympathy and consolation.

On very wet days we found the barn, with its massive beams and posts and high cobwebbed rafters, a fine place in which to let off steam. On the barn floor busy hens scratched with alternate claws, pecking, now and then, when the odd grain was uncovered. From time to time a bedraggled hen, feathers flattened by the rain, burst in through an aperture to join them. Mice scuttled across the floor or rustled in the bottom of the bays, while a farm cat sat motionless beside a mousehole, waiting to pounce. Outside, rain dripped from the eaves to splash in the shallow gutter worn by constant drips. We spent our time climbing the ladder to the high bays, to jump down to the various steps made by the sharp hayknives when cutting trusses for the animals. Over and over again we climbed for more and more jumps. The shallow steps were easy but the very deep ones tested our courage. For a change we played hide-and-seek in the hay, completely burying ourselves, to be found only when trodden on. Very occasionally we came upon a stolen, or unauthorised, hen's nest brim-full with eggs, and ran in great excitement to tell Mother.

We arrived home from school one day, to find ourselves each the proud owner of a small pony. What a delightful surprise! Sitting in the saddle and being led around the pasture was quite a new experience. Soon we were able to ride alone, cantering around just where the fancy took us.

When a friend called we had great fun putting a sack on one pony's back and, amidst much chatter and laughter, all climbing aboard. Round the field we cantered till the sack slipped, landing us all on the ground. We re-mounted again and again, for falling off provided the best fun of all.

Once we rode three aboard down a steep bank. Gradually we slipped forward till I, in front, landed on the pony's neck. I held my breath expecting the pony to lower its head and tip me off, but the stalwart beast bore the discomfort till we reached level ground and were able to wriggle back to our former positions. Mu and Kathleen, the blacksmith's daughter, rode their ponies over Disgwylfa Hill to Huntington school for music lessons, but mine never left the farm.

5. New Life on the Farm

Springtime on the farm was an exciting time for children, with many newborn creatures to fondle and caress. For adults it was a busy and anxious time, both with animals and poultry. Spring was lambing time, which for the men meant late nights and early mornings. With a storm lantern they made a careful search of secluded places, for ewes, when ready to lamb, often chose such places, and might be found to be in need of assistance.

Worst of all was damp, icy weather. Then we often saw a newborn lamb brought home, limp and chilled, and watched a hole being dug in the stable mixen and lined with a sack. Into this cosy nest the chilled lamb was put and covered with another sack. The mixen's generated heat soon revived the tiny mite.

Those more dead than alive were brought into the kitchen and laid on a folded sack on the warm hob. Some revived and were gradually fed with warm milk, others proved beyond recovery.

Occasionally a dead lamb was skinned and its pelt fitted, like a coat, to an orphan lamb. The dead lamb's mother was given time to get the scent of the pelt, when she would accept the orphan as her own. When no mother could be found for an orphan it became a tiddling, and was fed on cows' milk. Tiddlings became very tame and playful, following us around wherever we went.

Young lambs had many enemies. Foxes carried them off for their cubs, carrion crows, buzzards and ravens attacked them. Occasionally we were saddened to find a lamb with its eyes pecked out by crows, its anguished mother bleating piteously by its side.

Piglets were delightful little creatures, with pink bodies covered with silvery white hair. It was tempting to cuddle them too but when Mu caressed one against her cheek she was rewarded with a sharp nip, and was glad to drop it quickly.

The sow had her litter, usually at night, on a bed of straw in the cosy pigsty. While we were snug in bed, one of the men had to spend the night in the sty, with soft lantern light shining on the yellow straw and stone walls, for unless someone was present at the farrowing the clumsy sow would more than likely lie on a few piglets and crush them to death.

Piglets, like their mothers, were noisy creatures, squealing if touched. When they were chased, the old pigs' grunts sounded almost like a dog's bark, but when we scratched their backs with a stick they sounded almost like purring. Outside the sty they rooted up the ground with their snouts and had to be ringed. When the sharp points of the rings were forced through their snouts we covered our ears, for the piercing squeals grated on every nerve. Whenever we came upon them outside the sty they were munching with their noses to the ground, searching for food, but in hot weather they were to be found half-buried in squelchy mud by the lower pool, trying to keep cool.

We loved the baby calves and foals. They were so small, clean and brand-new-looking that we longed to pet and stroke them, but they shied away from every attempt. When a birth was expected in stable or byre a man stayed up all night to make sure there were no complications.

In the poultry domain Mother prepared for new arrivals. She placed hay in the goose-cubs, ready for the geese to make their nests. The cubs stood by the coal stack in the lean-to shed by the back door. We saw the geese steal in one by one to make their nests and later to lay an egg each day, covering it with hay and down from their breasts. When they were ready to sit, Mother closed their doors to leave them undisturbed. The slightest sound bothered them while they were sitting and our every visit to the coal stack earned a reproving hiss. The cub doors, perforated with large ventilation holes, were latched on the outside. When a goose needed to leave the nest to feed or to answer nature's call it tapped the door with its beak, and we were called by Mother to 'come and loose the goose out'. The goose announced her return by cackling gently, requesting her door to be closed.

For thirty days, while the eggs were incubating, the poor old gander wandered lone and dejected from one pond to the other, too indifferent even to hiss when we came close. Only when a goose left her nest to join him for a while did he show any animation.

After a month the eggs started bracking and soon the nests were full of fluffy yellow gullies. A couple of times each day Mother had to pill them, forcing open each small beak to push a couple of oatmeal pellets down the throat. We could not refrain from picking up the tiny balls of fluff and cuddling them, soft and warm, against our cheeks.

When the proud parents were allowed to leave the shed such a joyful cackling accompanied their reunion with the gander; with outstretched necks they exulted loud and long together. The goslings were introduced to the pond and were, at once, completely at home on the water.

Ganders were extremely savage creatures when protecting their young; with outstretched necks and hissing beaks they chased off all intruders.

Any creature unfortunate enough to get caught was flapped with steel-hard wings and pecked with a saw-edged beak. I was once a victim and never forgot the punishment dealt by those cruel wings. Ever after I gave the gander and his family a wide berth.

The goslings, roaming the pastures with their parents, soon learned to graze and needed little extra food. In autumn they wandered off to the stubbled cornfields and had to be called home with 'Gooze, gooze, gooze.' When found in a forbidden place they were driven out with the age-old rebuke, 'Shoo-lag! Shoo-lag!'

The ducks made their nests in the old house inglenook. Like geese they covered their eggs with down and straw. They laid nightly till their batch of eggs, from ten to thirty, had all been laid. Ducks were not ideal mothers, so a broody hen was usually employed to hatch a sitting of duck eggs. We were amused to watch the hen's anxiety when the brood first took to the water. To and fro she ran, close to the water's edge, desperately trying to coax her adventurous family back to dry land. In time, finding they came to no harm, she would wait with less agitation beside the pool.

In summer the ducks waddled off, in Indian file, down the lane to the Milw brook some quarter of a mile away. Each evening we called them home from the meadow's brow with 'Dill, dill, dill!' Invariably the drake quacked a loud acknowledgement and obediently led his wives home.

Turkeys laid as many as twenty eggs before they were ready to sit, and broody hens were engaged to help with the hatching. Young turkeys, or poults as they were called, were delicate creatures, prone to chills from damp and draughts. Often on dewy mornings we were sent to search for them in the damp grass, where they caught cramp or roup (a kind of purulent catarrh which made breathing difficult). Fortunately they grew hardier in time and needed less attention. They needed chopped greens with their mash and we children were sent to pick wormwood, which was a great favourite with them.

We kept our distance from the turkey-cocks, for they too could be savage when protecting their young and would stock any intruders. Turkey-cocks were proud birds, strutting about with feathers puffed, tails and wings fanned out, combs and wattles fiery red. After each strut they paused to gobble loudly. They were called with 'Pee, pee,' and like all domestic creatures recognised their own particular call.

We loved to cuddle the fluffy yellow chicks and ducklings, though this was not encouraged. In the coop the mother hen clucked anxiously, thrusting her head in and out between the bars, longing to be free. At the first sign of danger, perhaps the shadow of a hawk overhead, perhaps a carrion crow loitering with intent, or perhaps at the approach of a puppy or kitten, the mother's warning note brought her brood scuttling back to the safety of the coop. When allowed out, the mother hen accompanied her brood with fluffed-out feathers and slightly spread wings, clooking continually as she scratched with alternate claws to uncover titbits. When a tasty morsel was found she called them with a rapid 'Cook, cook, cook.' At the end of the day the chicks nestled in their mother's feathers. Now and then a tiny head popped out, but soon the mother's contented crooning purr lulled them all to sleep.

* * * *

With spring came the inevitable spring-cleaning, an upheaval scarcely less disruptive than house-moving. First the back-kitchen chimney had to be swept, a job usually done by the farm men. They brought no such refinements as poles and brushes to the task, but tied a suitably shaped gorse bush to the end of a long rope. This was fed down the chimney by a man on the roof to a couple inside, waiting to drag it down. Despite the protection of a dust-sheet, fixed over the front of the range, black dust escaped into the room and everything not previously removed had to be wiped over with a damp cloth. All was now ready for spring-cleaning.

Before the days of vacuum cleaners dust accumulated throughout the year in inaccessible places, for though housewives tried to lay the dust with damp tea-leaves before sweeping, clouds escaped to lodge behind heavy furniture too cumbersome to move regularly, and to settle on walls and ceilings and in various unreachable places.

One by one the rooms were stripped of all movable articles. Large, heavy furniture was moved away from walls. Ceilings and walls were brushed and, more often than not, papered or distempered. Cupboards and drawers were emptied, wiped out and relined with fresh paper, their contents overhauled and useless stuff discarded. Crockery from dresser shelves and cupboards was washed. All was in a hugger-mugger confusion and everyone's life thrown out of joint. One and all breathed a sigh of relief when life returned to normal and every room smelt sweet and clean.

* * * *

In late autumn or early winter the flocks had been brought down from the hills to be given extra nourishment in preparation for lambing and to be handy when it commenced. Sheep-cratches had been wheeled out to the pastures, to be replenished daily with hay, oats and cake.

Now, in late spring, with winter worries behind and the flock almost double its size, it was time to return them to the hills, to allow the grass to grow in the pastures. First of all the lambs had to be ear-marked to distinguish them from those of neighbours. All male lambs, with the exception, perhaps, of one or two choice ones fit to be selected for rams, had to be castrated.

Our castrator, a swarthy man with black curly hair, came of a musical family and given the opportunity would perhaps have made his mark in the world of music. Despite having had no tuition, he came in, clothes coated with grease, and made straight for the piano. There, like a man inspired, he played for several minutes, lost to the world, before remembering his mission, and taking his tools to join the men in the shed.

At dinner with the family he had many an amusing tale to tell. When Mother laughingly accused him of running off with her dishcloth on his previous visit he replied, 'Oh, that's nothing. I've run off with a lady's bodice since then!' He went on to relate how he had stayed overnight at a farm, rising before daybreak to catch a train. In the darkness he had donned a lady's bodice in mistake for his sleeved waistcoat, only discovering his mistake on reaching the station at daybreak. Each year his tales helped to enliven our pedestrian existence and were missed when a tool known as a bloodless castrator was introduced. This tool, like a broad-bladed pair of pincers, was shared with a neighbour and always referred to as 'the doings'.

Any sheep with dirty hindquarters were rounded up to be dagged (clipped) before returning them to the hill. Periodically throughout the summer they were gathered to be clipped again and treated with maggot-lotion to kill any eggs already laid and to deter the blow-fly. If enough eggs were laid and the animal left untreated the maggots would literally eat the animal alive.

Another hazard that needed attention was foot-rot. When more than one foot was affected with this painful disease the poor animal was obliged to kneel to graze. The diseased part of the hoof was cut away and the condition treated with a remedial lotion. When these various operations were carried out one of us children was called upon to 'keep the sheep up' in a corner.

6. The May Fair

The red-letter day in our childhood calendar was 17 May—the date of the Pleasure Fair at Hay. Before April was through it became the main topic of conversation both at home and at school. Over and over again we pictured the roundabouts and side-shows, the crowds and excitement, visualising them always under a blue sky. In the weeks preceding, when we met neighbours or adult friends, we were sure to be given a fairing, and as none of our immediate neighbours had children of their own to provide for in this respect, we were luckier than most of our friends.

One year, shortly before the Fair, Dad took us to the Far meadow to pick stones that might later damage the knives of the mowing machines. We were told that all the stones must be cleared or there'd be no Fair for us. We took that threat seriously. We sat on the banks bemoaning our lot, convinced that we'd never manage to clear the field in time. After a while I strolled disconsolately down to the lower half of the field and was surprised to find that completely free of stones. My heart leapt for joy! Racing back up the field I shouted the wonderful news. We set to work at once and, by the end of the day, the field was cleared.

That particular year we had been remarkably lucky with fairings and had collected five shillings between us. With what we already had in our money-boxes we had never been so rich. Talking it over, we agreed that Mother would probably be unwilling for so much to be squandered on amusements and decided to smuggle it to our bedroom and hide it for the great day.

When at last Fair Day arrived we each concealed several coins in our shoes before our purses were examined. Every step to the trap was torture! How thankfully we dropped on to the back seat. Mother climbed in the front and, gathering up the reins, Dad swayed the trap as he jumped in beside her. To the clarion call of the red cockerel on the mixen-top, we set off down the fold in high glee, scattering the white ducks waddling in our path, disturbing the pigs basking in the sunshine and the hens fluffing out their feathers in dust baths. The hawthorn hedges, bare for so long, were bursting into leaf, larch trees showed a veil of green, primroses starred the banks and cuckoos called unceasingly. In the stony lane the trap rocked from side to side on its springs, the pony tossing her head angrily as she slipped on the stones. Once on the road we kept a sharp lookout for our friends, Gladys and Gwen, wondering, as we rounded each bend, if we'd see them ahead. The whole, long, exciting day stretched out before us and evening seemed far away.

The countryside was deserted, for the Fair, like a vortex, drew people in from all sides. The dusty road, barred here and there with shadows, stretched invitingly ahead. Our happy hearts sang to the clip-clop of the pony's hoofs; the familiar smell of horseflesh and harness drifted back on the breeze. From time to time the pony snuffled through quivering lips, tossing her head and rattling her harness. She trotted on the flat and dropped to a walk on the hills; once on top, a flick of the reins set her trotting again. There was no one to be seen at Newgate Farm: the Evans family had already left for the Fair. Dad commented on the crops or the animals in the fields as we passed. How he could dwell on such mundane things on Fair Day was past our comprehension.

As we reached the brow of Clyro Hill the distant Black Mountains came into view. These mountains were our barometer: when they loomed close and every rock and ravine showed up clearly, we expected rain; when, as today, they appeared distant and hazy, it was a sure sign of fine weather. Far below, the Rive Wye looped through the valley like a silver snake, while white plumes of smoke puffed up from a train that threaded through the trees.

Beyond Pen-y-cae Farm we started the long descent to Clyro and Mother had to link her arm over the seat-back to prevent herself from slipping forward. There was no sign of life at Crossway so we guessed that Olwen and Trevor had already left with their parents. Crossfoot seemed deserted and Court Evan Gwyn stood silent behind its tumulus. Not a soul stirred in Clyro village, where the school, like our own, was closed for the Fair. Here, on lower ground, village gardens were bright with lilac and laburnum and the beech trees, under Cae-mawr, already bursting into brilliant leaf. On our left, as we left the village, Castle Tump rose steeply from the roadside. After climbing Longlands Pitch we dropped down Wyecliff Pitch and looked down on Hay, nestling in the valley beneath the foothills of the Black Mountains. We approached the Wye Bridge with quickening pulses, the music of the Fair swelling louder and louder to greet us. After pausing to pay toll at the end of the bridge we turned into the cobbled yard of the Black Swan, to be met by the acrid smell of stale beer, horse manure and urine. Alighting painfully, we sought a quiet corner in which to remove the coins from our shoes while our parents chatted with folks in the yard.

On the cobbles, on the far side of the street opposite the Black Swan, several traps rested on their shafts. Booths and stalls spread down from the

Hay-on-Wye.

clock tower and the street was thronged with people. There was no mistaking the country folk: their ruddy complexions, their gait, acquired by constant plodding over rough ground, their beaming faces flushed with pleasure at finding themselves amongst unaccustomed crowds all singled them out. They grouped together to chat, hailing each other in the local dialect.

‘’Ello, Jack, ke-ind weather for the fair, mun?’

‘Aye, it is, bo-ey, an’ by the look on it it’s set to last. I da’ like it when the ’ills do look near to, a long way off. It’s sure to rain then, you watch if I binna right!’

‘Look yender, mun, there’s ahld John The Bryn, stickin’ ’is chest out. ’E dunna ’alf think summat of ’isself, the silly ahld cooten.’

‘Aye, ’e’s pooty ’igh in the breastbon, in’t ’e? ’E fergets we knahs ’e was brought up on a mud floor. I canna think what makes ’m so fullish.’

By the clock tower we came upon our friends and our happiness was complete. The novelty of being in a crowd excited us. We hurried from stall to stall, trying to see everything at once. The crack of rifles guided us to the shooting galleries, where we found men levelling guns at moving targets or aiming at white balls rising and falling on jets of water. Nearby two farm hands stood chatting.

‘I ’ear you went to The Bryn sale, bo-ey. I warn there was a good dell there?’

‘Oh, aye, any a eft o’ people, mun. They made a smartish bit, no danger. ’Ow was it you didna come?’

‘Well, it ’a’ bin a busy wik on we, so I missed to go.’

‘What ya bin doin’, bo-ey?’

‘Oh, we ’a’ bin spreedin’ muck all the wik, but we got most on it sprod now.’

Beside a coconunt stall a swarthy woman with large dangling ear-rings stood by a box of wooden balls, inviting men to try their luck with the coconuts. Several had accepted the invitation and, with coat tails flying, hurled balls with great force at coconuts ground down in sawdust on wooden pedestals.

Nearby, a raucous voice called, ‘This way, folks! Pitch a ball in the bucket to win! Fourpence or a coconut!’ Demonstrating with what ease the prize could be won she threw ball after ball into an enamel pail. What an easy way to earn a few fourpences, we thought, and all had a try. But every ball we threw in bounced straight out again.

Across the street a loud voice enticed, ‘Walk up! Walk up! Every penny wins a prize!’ The gaudy prizes looked inviting, but feeling there was a catch here too, we refused to be tempted.

‘’Ow did you get ’ere so early, Jim?’ enquired a tall swarthy man of a fair young one.

‘Oh, Jones The Pentre puck me up in ’is trap. ’E ’ad a goodish load, too, but ’e squoze we all in.’

At the bell-ringing machine we found a crowd gathered to watch a brawny man in shirt sleeves swinging a heavy mallet to send a weight rushing up a groove to strike a bell at the top of a pole. As he exerted all his strength for a final swing a voice in the crowd exclaimed, ‘Lord, ahld Price is thrahin’ on it, now, in some form!’

‘Aye, ’e’s givin’ ’im chiack!’ added another.

The music of the steam organ drew us to where brightly coloured hobby horses with flaring nostrils rose and fell on their revolving platform. From the organ in the centre small colourful figures emerged to bang on drums and jerkily play various instruments in time with the music.

When the horses slowed down we plucked up courage to climb the steps to the vibrating platform to select a steed. I chose a low one, so Gwen was obliged to take a huge step to mount the high one alongside. Mu and Gladys found mounts some distance ahead. Slowly the platform moved, and as my horse rose Gwen’s fell. Many riders turned to wave at friends, but I felt none too secure on my nag's hard, slippery back and clung tightly to the spiral brass rod in front. The platform gathered speed; the faces of onlookers became blurred as we passed on our whirlwind way. In a few short minutes the platform steadied, the horses stopped and the ride was over.

At the foot of the steps several giggling girls with vivid scarlet lips swaggered past a group of young men, throwing them saucy glances. Unimpressed, one of the men commented, 'Lord, look at them ahld wenches, they 'anna 'alf raddled their chops.'

None of us was brave enough to try the high chair-o-plane chairs, swinging obliquely from their umbrella-like roof, but several adventurous folk seemed to be enjoying the experience.

Across the street, on the Blue Boar corner, two women met:

''Ello, Mrs Price, 'ow be you today?'

'Oh, I do feel right ordinary, some road. I canna think what ails me.'

'No, you 'anna bin lookin' right for some time. Why not come and stop with we for a bit? A change will make the back on you. Oh, 'ere's Mrs Pugh. 'Ello, Mrs Pugh. 'Ave you 'eard any news of Mrs Davies The Wern?'

'Aye, I did go a purpose journey to see 'er about three o'clock yesterday evenin'. 'Er was up in 'er sittin's, then, so 'er'll be down in a day or two, sure to. I warn you 'eard as Meredith The Cwm 'ad gone?'

'Aye, what did come to 'im, for 'im to go so simple?'

'I da' knah no aim, but 'im was only bad for a day or two.'

The switchbacks were great fun: the four of us were able to share one seat. Up and down the hills we flew, and what a thrill the downward slope provided! Screams of laughter echoed around. With legs too short to reach the floor I clung tightly to the horizontal bar. By the time the ride was over my arms ached unbearably.

'Well, Mary, be you enjoyin' the fair?' enquired a man of a pretty fair-haired child. 'I be, up to yet, thank you,' was her reply.

We thoroughly enjoyed our tea in the black and white café with its oak beams and posts and sloping oak floors. Across the square screams of laughter came from the swing-boats and, tea over, we hurried out to join in the fun. We climbed into the first available boat and, sitting opposite each other, crossed ropes before pulling alternately to send each other flying high and plunging swiftly downwards. It was exhilarating to sail high over the heads of the onlookers, till the motion of the swing made me sick: the showman had to be called to run his plank under the boat so I could disembark and stand greenfaced by to watch the others' fun.

Beside me two young men were trying to persuade a couple of lassies to join them for a ride. 'Come on, you can sit anunt we,' one coaxed. 'We're particular who we ride with,' came the haughty reply. 'Come on, da be so ognel: you binna too big-sorted to ride with we, be yer?'

Before the day was through we had bought brandy-snaps, we had rolled pennies on numbered squares, we had thrown hoops on to pegs and hooked ducks off water, but had little to show for our pains and pennies.

As daylight faded, naphtha flares brought an intimate cosiness to the streets. Sweethearts, too shy to be seen together in daylight, started pairing up. But our Fair Day was over. Reluctantly we accompanied our parents to the trap, calling *en route* at the draper's, where we found a woman of our acquaintance endeavouring to purchase a bow-tie.

'I wants a bah—tie,' she informed the assistant. Again and again she unsuccessfully repeated the request. Finally, in desperation, she indicated the base of her throat with her index finger. 'I wants a bah-tie to putt 'ere,' she reiterated. The assistant got the message.

At the Black Swan the passage was crowded with men talking and arguing, each with a mug of beer in his hand, while a thick haze of tobacco smoke hung below the ceiling. The pony was harnessed to the trap, and with her head turned toward home needed no urging. Several other families were also leaving, and trap after trap rumbled over the bridge.

Hay-on-Wye.

Older pedestrians, wearied with the noise and excitement, toiled up Wye Cliff Pitch, clutching the hands of children reluctant to leave. From the back seat of the trap we watched the lights of the Fair dim with distance and heard its music slowly die away.

The long climb to the top of Clyro Hill was a strain on the pony, so Mother and Dad sat forward to 'help the mare and keep the shafts down'. On the crest of the hill bare trees were etched in a fretwork of twigs against the pale evening sky. Behind us the Black Mountains and Brecon Beacons were sharp-edged, in bold relief. The air grew colder with every mile. From the top the pony trotted the whole way, to be greeted on arrival by the farm dogs barking madly until their wagging tails told us we were recognised. All evening we talked of nothing but the Fair, and during the following week relived the happy day over and over again.

* * * *

In conjunction with the Pleasure Fair on 17 May there was a Hiring Fair, and in the days preceding, masters and men bargained over the subsequent year's hire. A good man was invited to stay on and, in some cases, was offered a small rise as an inducement to stay. For the lazy and incompetent it was time to pack their tin trunks and seek labour elsewhere. Some men preferred a change of district and left to try their fortunes further afield.

On Fair morning men and maids were paid their yearly wages, minus some small advances that had been requested during the year. Having worked from early morning till late evening for a whole year, with the exception of Sunday evenings, they had at last earned a week's holiday. For the past year their needs had been few. Food and shelter had been provided, and there was little in the depths of the country on which to spend their money. At Fair time they fitted themselves out with any items of clothing needed to see them through the next twelve months, and except for a little pocket-money, their year's wage would be put by. By today's standards they were far from rich, earning 25 shillings a week (£1.25), but they knew the long-lost secret of how to be happy and contented on little—for happy and contented most of them were, many managing to save enough after a few years to rent a cottage or smallholding and settle down to wedded bliss.

On Fair morning they had little to pack: their only decent suit would be worn. Waggoners, shepherds and cowherds wore marks of distinction to advertise their skills. At one time maids wore aprons to the Fair, removing them when they were hired. It was not uncommon on Fair Day to see a young lad, leaving home for the first time, standing self-consciously on the pavement beside his tin trunk, waiting to be hired. Lost and bewildered, he no doubt wondered what the future held for him, what kind of a place his new home would be, how he would be treated.

When Dad was hiring a new waggoner we were always curious to find what kind of a person he'd turn out to be. One year the new man had extremely loose teeth: so loose were they that he daren't open his mouth, properly, to speak, lest he should lose them altogether. One day, while he was eating rice pudding, they fell out into his plate, forcing him to fish them out and clap them back into his mouth. We children exploded with laughter and earned a sharp reprimand from Dad, though he had considerable difficulty in keeping his own composure.

For many years we had the same conscientious waggoner, Ernie, who had a keen sense of humour and kept us highly entertained at meal-times with tales of past and current experiences. Before we had even heard the tale, we were convulsed by his infectious chortles; by the time the story was finally told, our sides ached.

For many years Ernie had no girl-friend. When we ragged him about this his answer was, 'Well, them do say that there's a crah [crow] for every crah, but I'm afraid mine was shot in the cornfield.' However, Ernie finally found his mate, and they built a nest together.

7. Summer Days

We'll talk of sunshine and of song,
Of summer days when we were young,
Sweet childish days that were as long
As twenty days are now.

William Wordsworth

Whenever possible each sunny summer day was spent outdoors. Very hot weather drove us from our exposed playhouse to the cool green shade of the sycamore tree on the bank behind the house. There we nursed our dolls in 'arm-chairs' formed by exposed roots, our backs against the trunk. Overhead innumerable bees buzzed in the scented foliage. Breezes stirred the leaves, to send patches of sunlight dancing across the grass and greenish yellow petals fluttering down to form a carpet all around.

Early summer brought shearing-time and an element of excitement, for neighbours arrived to lend a helping hand. From our shady bank we watched dogs and men on horse-back bound for Newchurch Hill to gather the flock for washing. After a time, distant bleating, raised voices and yapping dogs could be heard gradually growing louder and louder, till the flock could be seen fanning out over the bank above the well, to be rounded up by the dogs and headed down the lane for the Milw brook.

All the noise and excitement prompted us to leave our leafy shade to follow and watch, though we had seen it all before. The brook had been stanked up to form a deep pool, and a large pen of hurdles erected for the sheep. From the main pen a narrow pen led to the pool. A few sheep at a time were ushered into the narrow pen and thrown, one by one, into the pool and well doused under the water with a wooden paddle before each animal dragged its heavy body out on the far side, shaking its saturated fleece and spraying water in all directions. By the time the job was completed men and dogs were almost as wet as the sheep.

An early start was made on shearing days to sweep the barn, set out the shearing benches and put salt or disinfectant to hand, in case of accidental cuts. At this time of year the fleece rose from the back of the sheep, making clipping easier. If the day turned out wet the operation had to be postponed, for wet fleeces clung to the shears, making the job impossible.

Soon neighbours began arriving as we stood shyly by, knowing each would have a few words for us and perhaps even a coin or two. Some set their sheep on the floor and bent over them to shear, while others used the benches provided. It was one man's job to catch the sheep, while another rolled up the fleeces ready for the woolsacks.

As dinnertime approached each man completed the animal in hand, and all clattered into the kitchen and queued up at the sink to wash their hands before settling down at the table. The meal was accompanied by roars of laughter as tales were told and gossip exchanged. The meal over, all rose as one and clattered out to resume their work, leaving behind a profound stillness broken only by the tick of the clock.

At the end of the long day the thin-looking, milk-white sheep were reunited with their lambs, and the deafening bleating that had persisted throughout the day slowly subsided and peace reigned once more. But the noisiest time of all was weaning time, when bleating continued for days before the parting was finally accepted.

At the first opportunity the huge woolsacks, opening along the long edge, were strung up by ropes to a beam. One of us children was lifted into the sack to tread the fleeces well down into the corners, and the bulging sacks were sewn together with a large sacking needle threaded with string.

In a day or two the sheep were rounded up to be branded with pitch. The pitch bucket containing solid, shining, black pitch in which the branding-irons had set, was heated over the kitchen fire to a thick, boiling, bubbling consistency, with a healthy tar-like smell. As it was rushed out to where the sheep were gathered in the shed one of us children was called to 'mind the door', opening it to release each sheep as it was pitched.

Again the sheep were gathered for dipping to prevent sheep-scab, an extremely infectious disease which could soon decimate a flock. Dipping was compulsory. The local bobby had to be notified to attend, and the dipping-tub, used by all neighbouring farmers, had to be reserved. A lotion was stirred into the water to impregnate the fleece and provide a year's protection against the disease.

When the excitement of shearing was over we found the garden a place well worth visiting. Pea-pods were bursting with succulent peas and bushes laden with ripe juicy gooseberries and red and black currants. Later in the season just the thought of plums made our mouths water. So easy to climb, the Victoria plum tree spread a branch conveniently over the privy roof on which we could sit completely hidden from view while feasting on the luscious plums within easy reach. When Mother called a quick dash was made to a more innocent part of the garden.

The privy, screened in front by bushes, was almost entirely covered by a mock-orange shrub. In summer I loved to steal away to its sun-dappled step to read. Now the evocative scent of orange blossom wings my thoughts to that childhood haunt and those halcyon days, seen, through the mellowing mists of time, as wholly idyllic.

When we were children it was considered highly improper for a woman to enter a privy while there were men about. Usually the wood-pile was conveniently placed so that should a man appear unexpectedly when a woman was thither bound she could innocently turn aside for a bundle of sticks, busying herself at the wood-pile until the coast was clear.

Of course in those days all houses in remote country districts had outside privies. It was not until 1939, shortly before the outbreak of the Second World War, that flush toilets first came to our area when council houses were built in the neighbouring village of Gladestry. The first houses to be built in the area in living memory, they provided immense interest for old and young alike. When the houses were finally completed one old stager, concerned to find no privies in the gardens, exclaimed, 'Well, them 'anna putt nerra consarn in the ge-ardens.' When he was told the houses had indoor lavatories he was thunderstruck. 'What! In the house? Well, that canna be 'ealthy.'

* * * *

In late April the fields being kept up for hay were cleared of animals. Later they were chain-harrowed to level the oonti-tumps and to spread the manure left by the animals. They were also cleared of stones, which might later damage the mowing machine knives.

In early July preparations for haymaking began in earnest. The mowing machine was overhauled and its knives gripped in the vice to be sharpened. Rakes were examined and new teeth made for the gaps left by the previous year's wear.

By now the meadow grass was tall and thick and silvered in the downsweep of the wind. The high feathery grass, of every conceivable shade of green, was bright with flowers of every hue. There were big white moon-daisies, yellow buttercups, blue scabious, yellow rattle, birdsfoot trefoil, meadowsweet, hawkweed, cranesbill and many more. Amongst them all we loved to search for the distinctive quaking grass and, when no adult was about, play hide and seek in the fragrant carpet.

Countrymen were always conscious of weather changes and we were used to hearing such phrases as, 'It oona rain till the sun gets round to the butt of the wind.' Or, 'The wind is goin' back agen the sun, so it's sure to rain.' At harvest time the moon was studied with extra care and the coming weather predicted by its position and tilt in the sky. When this was favourable and the mountains distant and hazy, a spell of settled weather was expected and a start could be made on the hay.

The first task was to cut by hand a wide swath around the field to accommodate the mowing machine. Then scythes were sharpened and their blades tested with the thumb, making a pinging sound. Step by step the fragrant grass fell to the long sibilant sweep of the scythe.

Early next day, as the sun cast long dewy shadows and pale shafts of light between the trees, the waggoner, with his horse and machine, made for the meadow, leaving dark trails across the dewy pasture. Soon the whirr of the machine could be heard—a special summer sound, evoking mental pictures of sun-gilded, dew-pearled mornings that heralded long, happy, carefree days. On his hard, fan-patterned, metal seat, the waggoner looked alarmingly insecure as the machine bumped and rocked over the uneven ground. Round and round the horse plodded, till swath after swath lay dark on the ground. At midday the horse was unhooked and, with gears a-jangling, thankfully reached the pool for a long cold drink, returning then to the stable for a bait and a rest.

In hot weather the swaths were soon ready for turning with hand-rakes to bring the damp hay uppermost. Every available hand was enlisted. The farm men turned the hay expertly and quickly as they walked along, leaving the novices far behind, often with blistered hands. As the sun reached its zenith, and shadows became dark pools at the workers' feet, perspiration oozed from every pore and hayseeds clung to the sweat, irritating sunburned skin. Next, the swath-turner scattered the hay from the heavy swaths, to make in the sun, before it was raked into light windrows, through which the breeze could pass to dry it thoroughly. Now all hands were needed to pile it into cocks ready for hauling.

The vehicle used for this purpose was a two-wheeled waggon known as a gambo, which had a tall cart-stick at either corner and small gate-like bars above the wheels. As soon as it was brought from the wainhouse, Mu and I rushed to the fold for the shaky ride to the meadow. The empty gambo bumped and rattled its way over the rutted ground; the pikles jumped and jarred on its floor; our lips trembled, our teeth chattered and our very innards quivered as the wooden, iron-rimmed wheels rumbled along. In the meadows churring grasshoppers and tiny yellow frogs hopped about in the yellowish-green aftermath. We dived into the haycocks, rolled down the banks and gambolled about until the day came when we, too, were able to take a share in the work.

We envied the loader riding along on the gambo. To us his job seemed child's play, but there was quite an art in arranging a load, for each forkful had to be carefully placed and held in position by the subsequent one. A load carelessly arranged soon fell to pieces when jolting over uneven ground.

The old horse hung its head while flies settled in small black heaps in the pus in the corners of its half-closed eyes. The poor animal was constantly plagued by horseflies, twitching its ears, swishing its tail, stamping its feet and puckering its skin against them. We fed it wisps of hay to try to take its mind off them.

When the load was completed it was roped down for the bumpy journey home. A second horse was untied from the hedge and hitched to the traces. Axles creaked as the heavy gambo lumbered forward, rocking from side to side and brushing the high hedge, where it left wisps of hay hanging from the branches.

In the farmyard the huge, high barn doors were opened at either side to allow the horses to pass straight through and draw the load into the centre, to be unloaded into the bays. When the hay reached the eaves we children had to mye it under the sloping roof. This we did by clinging to the beams and thrusting it in with our feet. It was stifling hot under the burning tiles.

After we had toiled the whole afternoon the arrival of tea was a welcome sight. Everyone made for the shady hedge and lay back in the cool grass while the picnic was spread. Then back to work till the sun dropped behind the horizon, leaving the meadow pleasantly cool, with gentle air hardly stirring the topmost leaves. Evening stillness was broken only by the distant lowing of cows waiting to be milked, and voices wafting across the valley from the haymakers in Dolbedwen meadow. At dewfall we wearily followed the last load home, accompanied, perhaps, by the churring of the night-jar.

Back in the farmyard leathern bats dived and swooped with small squeaks of excitement or frustration. We were amazed to learn that these creatures suckled their young and that, even as they flew, their naked babies clung to their bodies. Night after night we tried to knock one down with long sticks for a closer look, but all to no avail. On those summer nights we drifted into sleep to the distant 'rerp rerp' of the corncrake, borne from distant fields on the quiet evening air.

When the field had been cleared, stray wisps were gathered with the horse-rake. One year I was permitted to load the rakings. Only then did I discover how difficult it was to arrange the load and at the same time keep one's balance. I was warned to take care and not to get jolted off as the gutter was crossed, but before I even reached it I found myself, and half my load, on the ground. Was my face red?

Another unpleasant experience, I recall, was being told to lead the front horse up the steep bank towards the meadow gate, with a heavy load. Timidly I took the rein at arm's length. The horse, no doubt, sensed my fear and incompetence, and a sudden move I made startled it and it stopped pulling. The horse in the shafts was unable, alone, to hold the heavy load, and it ran back down the bank taking the horses with it. The loader, who had elected to ride home on the load, jumped clear and, luckily, escaped unhurt. I stood rooted to the spot, expecting a major disaster, and was never more relieved than to see the gambo come to a halt on flat ground, still upright.

When the hay had all been carted in good weather everyone was in high spirits, but unfortunately there were many summers when it had to be turned repeatedly as the fitful sun dried it between showers. August days were often oppressive: too languorous even for birds to sing. Anxious eyes searched the sky as mountains loomed closer and sounds became magnified. Threatening clouds billowed up; there was not a breath of air; everyone felt on edge. A sudden breeze, a few large spots of rain and a distant rumble of thunder heralded a storm. Everyone rushed for shelter. In the house all mirrors were covered against lightning and windows were opened for thunderbolts to escape. Dogs, which normally refused to enter the house, rushed in to crouch trembling beside their master. Mu and I hid under the stairs, away from the lightning flashes and winced at every crack of thunder. In the vertical downpour, large spots pitted the pools and gathered dust globules in the fold. The thunder moved away only to return before the storm finally cleared, leaving the air light and fresh, the fold smelling of dust and everyone feeling relaxed. The hay had been drenched, however, and would take days to dry.

It was tempting, in a poor season, to cart hay not thoroughly dry but this courted disaster. Damp hay turned mouldy in the bays and could even heat to such an extent that it burst into flames.

It was during haymaking time in 1926 that we saw our first aeroplane. It was dinnertime and the kitchen door wide open. A low, droning, throbbing sound, quite alien to the countryside, came closer and closer. Whatever could it be? Everyone rushed out and there, sailing high in the sky, was an aeroplane. What an excitement! Our cousin Idris, up from the mining valleys during the General Strike, threw the dregs from his teacup. To everyone's amusement the cup parted company with the handle, which was all he had left to take indoors.

8. Autumn

Almost before haymaking was over the cornfields were harvest-ripe. By now the air held a touch of autumn. Soft mists rose from the valleys and morning dew had a crisp suggestion of frost. Golden autumn sun shone through thin mists on hedgerows bright with maturing fruit. Out of a purple evening haze an enormous moon rose over the crest of the hill to hold us spellbound. Harvest time had arrived.

In the early days scythes were honed to razor-sharpness before setting out for the cornfields. The reapers moved in a slanting line, keeping the same distance apart. Before the long, rhythmic sweeps of the scythes the standing corn fell with a ripping, rasping sound. From time to time a halt was called to stretch aching backs and whet blunting blades. Hour after hour they laboured, with sleeves rolled up, neck bands open and flannel shirts working out of trouser tops. Women were enlisted to bind the sheaves and set them up in stooks to dry and ripen in the sun. Corn was cut before it was fully ripe, so that the grains would not fall from the ears in the handling. The stooked sheaves were left for a fortnight or more to dry and ripen before hauling. If crops were extra heavy, ricks were built in the fields and thatched with straw, plaited and twisted into a tight waterproof covering to keep the corn dry throughout the winter.

Later, with the inception of the reaping machine, scythes were discarded. The sails of the reaper passed over the standing corn, bringing it down on to a moving canvas, where it was cut and passed out on to the stubble to be bound. The reaper was superseded by the binder-reaper, which not only cut the corn but bound it into sheaves, ejecting each tied sheaf on to the stubble with a kind of kicking prong. On a golden autumn day a cornfield was a picturesque scene. Stooks, like small tents, dotted the stubble in even rows, while spirited horses drew the binder with sails turning under a blue sky.

The binder was a temperamental machine and parts worked loose or broke on the rough ground. Harvest was held up while the blacksmith repaired the damage or made a new part. Men became anxious and frustrated, fearing the weather would break. The stubbled oat-stalks made long white scratchmarks on our sunburnt arms; they scratched and stabbed our legs too, sometimes drawing blood.

The clanking, rattling machine terrified the rabbits in the corn, forcing them to retreat further and further into the centre of the patch. As it grew smaller the farm dogs whimpered, sensing the rabbits' nearness. When the patch became too small for further concealment terrified rabbits dashed out in all directions. Men shouted, guns fired and dogs gave chase, tossing the squealing rabbits into the air. Few managed to escape. Mu and I were desperately sorry for the poor bunnies but knew they had to be destroyed, for they played havoc with the farm crops.

When the bright September harvest moon rose in a clear sky for a few consecutive nights, providing ample light by which to work, harvesting continued long after dark in the pleasantly cool night air. Pale shadows were thrown on the whitened stubble; outlines of trees and hedges were vague and insubstantial, and the laughing voices of unseen people wafted from distant fields. Moonlight's unearthly radiance lent romance to the scene.

Fowlhouses were hauled to the cleared stubble, where undersown clover was already springing green, for the hens to feast on the fallen grain.

* * * *

September was also the climax of the shepherd's year, when sheep were selected, trimmed and coloured to look their best at the ewe sales. Before the days of stock-lorries, drovers made a very early start on sale day for a leisurely drive to the market. Roads were full of bleating sheep, barking dogs and shouting men. Children were enlisted to stand at road junctions to head the sheep in the right direction. Crowded pens displayed fleeces of a score of different colours, amongst which farmers, young and old, passed to admire and criticise by turn. Yapping dogs threatened to drown the auctioneer's voice, though some crouched, nose on paws, ready to spring into action at their owner's command.

For the pony sales munts and their foals were rounded up on the hills on horseback. Unused to human contact they were exceedingly wild and difficult to collect. Everyone available was employed to stand at strategic points, waving their arms and shouting, to head them in the right direction. On this day the countryside echoed to the sound of clip-clopping hoofs as bunch after bunch headed for the horse-fair at Huntington, just over the English border.

* * * *

There was a sense of relief when the harvest was safely gathered, and work proceeded at a more leisurely pace. By now the hillside bracken was rusty-brown and men busied themselves in cutting and hauling it for winter bedding.

The harvesting of root-crops was viewed with less urgency. The whole family turned out for the back-breaking job of potato-picking and all were heartily glad to see the last load of bulging sacks on its way to the cellar store. Turnips, swedes and mangolds were topped, butted and thrown into heaps ready to be carted to cootches and covered with straw and bracken against winter frosts.

Autumn days were nutting days. With baskets and hooked sticks Mu and I set out for the high hazel hedges between fields. Along arable headlands, brightened with pimpernel, mayweed and persicaria, many sheelers already lay on the ground. Others, still on the branches, needed but a slight shake to bring them showering around us. Running along the branches, his bushy tail erect, we espied the red squirrel gathering his winter store, and from a pile of leaves, where he had dozed in the sun, a hedgehog sleepily emerged to eat all he could in readiness for his long winter's sleep. Nose down, along the hedge-bank, a brown weasel tracked its prey. So engrossed was he that we got quite close before being noticed; then, sitting upright in the grass, he examined us intently for a moment with his sharp, bright eyes, before hurrying on his way.

Each year, accompanied by Mother or Granny, we skipped down the lane to Cae Milw to pick blackberries from the hedges and bramble banks. In the brook, beneath the alders, cows twitched and swished their tails, their eyes staring unseeingly ahead. A cloud of insects danced above the water. Often in Cae Milw we heard the green woodpecker's yaffling cry and caught a brief glimpse of its green and yellow plumage and red cap as we followed its undulating flight. Here too a grey and white heron followed the brook on slow, heavy wings, uttering its harsh 'kronk kronk', its neck drawn back between its shoulders, its legs straight out behind. Mother called it a crane and said it went up the brook to bring down the rain.

Throughout this season subtle changes were taking place. Trees withdrew their sap and earth's pulses gradually slowed down for winter's sleep. Birds flew in flocks from place to place, restless with thoughts of migration. Swallows gathered on barn tops and, urged by some impulse, followed the swifts to warmer climes.

Men now found time to attend to broken hedges. Ditches, choked by leaves and rubbish, were cleared ready for winter's rain. Gorse was burned on the hill to clear the ground; coal and cider were carted; winter logs were sawn on the horse at the woodpile. We children accompanied

Mother and Granny to bring home apronsful of kindling wood and tushed bundles of long sticks behind us.

Soon equinoctial gales stripped leaves from the trees, whirling them high in the air. In the rickyard loose straw was whisked high on the gusts. Birds were blown hither and thither and matronly hens with ruffled feathers squawked with indignation at the buffeting they received. But Mu and I found it great fun to gambol, shout and battle against the gusts that buffeted our faces, snatched away our breath and whisked our skirts around our ears; then we'd turn and lean against the wind to be carried along.

The old roadman persuaded us that the wind had once got under his cape and carried him across the valley from the Little Mountain to Newchurch Hill. We could hardly wait to try this out ourselves. Donning our capes we climbed the steep bank to where the gale roared through the sycamore, bending and tossing its branches and scattering leaves to right and left. Up there the wind was rather frightening. Of course, we only wanted to be carried across the narrow dingle to our playhouse but could we be sure that the wind would drop us there? Once airborne we feared we'd be at the wind's mercy and there was no telling where we'd eventually touch down. Half-heartedly we spread our capes, then when nothing happened we became more daring, flapping our arms to lift the capes and eventually jumping high to give the wind a helping hand. All to no avail—we remained firmly on the ground and hardly knew whether to be glad or sorry.

With the arrival of autumn rains, gateways were soon churned into mud pools by animal's feet—thick, squelching mud that threatened to suck the boots from the feet. In the fold, summer's dust also changed to thick mud, which had periodically to be scraped away with the mud-scraper. A heap of bracken was placed by the boot-scraper and old sacks laid by the doorstep for wiping muddy boots. In such weather men went to work with sacks over their shoulders, secured by a nail at the front. A second sack, tied around the waist with binder-twine, protected the thighs. Their old felt hats, wet through by the end of the day, had to be dried out overnight.

In very wet weather indoor jobs were found for the men, for they were never kept idle. Each job was accompanied by happy whistling. Women never whistled, for 'twas said:

A whistling girl and a crowing hen
is neither good to God or men.

* * * *

Threshing Day

Like shearing day, threshing day held an element of excitement for us, with neighbours again arriving to assist. The steam engine and threshing drum travelled from farm to farm, each of the two farms involved providing a couple of horses for the journey. As each machine weighed a couple of tons or more they provided a severe test for the horses on steep gradients.

Our men usually collected the tackle from Blaencerdi, a farm some half a mile beyond the village and the home of our friends Gladys and Gwen. The narrow road, very steep in places, wound downhill all the way from Blaencerdi to the village, so a metal, boat-shaped device, known as a slipper, was attached to the rear wheels to act as a brake.

On our side of the village the road again climbed steeply for several hundred yards, and extra horses had to be hitched to the traces. Then, to the accompaniment of clanking gears, tossing heads and snuffling lips, the command to move was given, 'Come, Bonnie! Blossom! Duke! Brown!' With their great necks arched downward and clouds of vapour rising from their nostrils the horses strained forward, their hoofs striking sparks from the road as they strove to gain a foothold. The men, with hard-edged voices, ran beside them, urging them on, while someone with a chock in each hand followed closely to squat up the wheels when a halt was called. The huge machine filled the narrow road and anything encountered had to reverse to the nearest gateway to allow it to pass.

Everyone breathed a sigh of relief when the lane gate was reached without incident, but the final steep climb up the fold was the trickiest part of all. To turn the wainhouse corner the horses had to be kept going at full speed to climb the hill, while at the same time the front horse had to be led forward, in a straight line, almost into the pig-sty door, before the machine was in the right position to turn the corner. Too sharp a turn would have overturned it on to the mixen.

The following morning an early start was made to fill the huge water-butt ready for the thirsty engine and carry coal for the hungry fire. Soon the engine driver arrived to get his fire started. As he fed his furnace, heat soared upwards, shimmering and distorting every object beyond. A wide belt stretched from the large engine fly-wheel to the small wheel of the drum. As the engine roared into life it sent the hens, pecking around the corn-bays, clucking and cackling, half flying, half running, to the rickyard gate and safety.

Soon neighbours arrived, and after a short chat took up their positions for the day. One or two climbed the long ladder to the high bay, to pass sheaves to the man on the drum. Here, twine which bound each sheaf was cut and the loose straw fed into the whirring machine where the grain was separated from the straw and husks, to emerge through outlets at the rear. The straw, disgorged at the side of the drum, was pitched to an empty bay for men to distribute evenly. The husks also soon formed a pile that had to be carried away. It was one man's job to attend to the sacks, fixed on hooks, at the outlets. As each sack became full he closed the outlet door, exchanged an empty sack for a full one and, bending almost double under its weight, made his way to the granary to empty the corn in a golden pile upon the floor.

Throughout the day men's voices were raised above the constant chugging and whirring. Threshing was dusty work; clothes became white and nostrils black with dust. The poor man on the drum fared worst of all; his hair, eyelashes and eyebrows were white with clinging dust.

Towards the end of the day a great deal of shouting and barking accompanied the killing of rats. When the final sheaves were removed there was no hiding place. Rats dashed out in all directions. Some were caught by dogs, some stunned by the men and some escaped to breed another day.

9. Winter

As the cold intensified, milking-cows and cart horses were housed for the winter. It was about this time of the year that the rabbit-catcher arrived with his ferrets, nets and wires. He lived in, and stayed a week or more. He kept his ivory-coloured, pink-eyed ferrets in a box in the shed. Through the netting front we watched them pacing from side to side, raising their heads to sniff the air.

Skilled at his job, the rabbit-catcher knew just where to find the rabbit runs, for rabbits were creatures of habit, following fixed paths to their feeding-grounds. The wires, tied with a slip-knot, were fixed a short distance from the burrow, just where the rabbit was gathering speed.

At first light each morning the catcher went round his wires, coming home laden with rabbits. Any that escaped the wires were caught with nets which were placed over every outlet from a warren, before the ferret was released down one of the holes. As rabbits sensed the ferret's approach they dashed for the nearest exit, only to become entangled in the net. Occasionally the ferret came upon an unsuspecting rabbit, instantly killing it and settling down to a tasty meal followed by a cosy nap. When, after some time, it failed to return, the catcher released a second ferret attached to a length of cord to locate its mate, listening, with his ear to the hole, for their squeaks as they greeted each other, thereby trying to establish their position. He then withdrew the second ferret by the cord and dug down to where he assessed the other ferret to be. If this failed, he could repeat the procedure, or just wait for it to show up when its nap was over. By the end of the catcher's stay, rows and rows of rabbits hung in pairs from poles in the shed, waiting for market-day.

Lengthening days brought colder weather. Rime frosted roof and ground, and the air was keen and cold. Men tied twine around their coats against the bitter wind and thumped their arms across their chests to keep the blood moving. Hands became numbed and clumsy; painful chaps opened on dry, calloused skin, to weep and bleed. Ice on ponds had to be broken for animals to drink. As grass disappeared, men, almost buried by trusses of hay, struggled to the fields to fodder ragged-coated animals whose flanks were caked with dry mud and dung.

Night skies blazed with stars like sparkling gems. Bright moonlight incited cockerels to answer each other from farm to farm. Dogs 'bayed the moon', forcing Ernie to rise from his bed with harsh reprimands so that all might get to sleep.

At this time of year, on the waxing of the moon, the pig was killed. When the sad day arrived Mu and I ran to hide and cover our ears against the squeals and snorts that rent the air, as the poor pig, now almost too fat to waddle, was hauled and pushed to the slaughter-bench. Several hands held it down while the razor-sharp knife was plunged into the throat and blood gushed out into the bucket placed beneath the bench. Thankfully, death came quickly. Boiling water was poured over the carcass, the outer layer of the trotters was peeled off and the skin scraped clean, to leave a spotless pig, blotched pink from the scalding water. A notched wooden arm called a gambrel was thrust through the tendons of the back legs near the knee joint and the heavy carcass strung up to a beam in the shed. Then it was cut down the front, from tail to snout, and disembowelled.

It was Mother's job to remove the fat that encased the intestines and render it down to make delicious scratchings which left behind the finest lard. Tasty faggots and haslet were made from the various organs. The pig's fry, steaks and spare-rib were delicious. Much of this was shared with neighbours, who later returned the compliment.

When the pig was being cut up Mu and I had to take turns in holding the lantern or candle. We heartily disliked this job, which meant leaving a favourite hobby in the warm kitchen to stand in the cold, draughty shed, with freezing hands and feet, trying to throw a glimmer on the vital spot and repeatedly getting into trouble for not holding it steady. After several warnings Dad would lose patience and angrily say, 'Well, name o' goodness, hold the thing steady!' He was always touchy on these occasions and though we failed to realise it, probably hated his cold job as much as we did ours.

The hams, shoulders and flitches were carried into the dairy and laid on the salting-stone. Mother rubbed them with saltpetre, covered them with salt and left them for about three weeks to cure. The salt was bought in large slabs or bars and had to be cut up and crushed before use. At the appropriate time the bacon was lifted from the stone and brushed free of salt. The hams and shoulders were hung on sturdy hooks from the kitchen ceiling, with stout brown paper attached at the bottom to catch the occasional salty drip. The flitches were placed on layers of paper on meat cratches, also suspended from the ceiling. Bacon was the family's main meat: it was fried for breakfast, boiled for dinner and often eaten cold for supper.

With winter's snow came silence. Distant mountains rose like white marble against a leaden sky. Banks and hollows levelled out, footpaths disappeared. Men turned out with picks and shovels to open blocked roads. Wild animals, driven by hunger, ventured near the house. Boots, saturated by plodding hour after hour through snow and slush, had to be dried out overnight on the hob. By morning they were board-hard, and forcing them on feet swollen with chilblains which were often broken and weeping brought tears to the men's eyes.

Sheep, sensing a storm, came down from the high ground in search of shelter. Ironically, screaming winds often blew the snow from the exposed paths into the very nooks they had chosen for refuge, thereby burying them. In blizzard conditions men trudged through deep snow in search of them, armed with shovels and poles to prod the snow and locate the soft bodies beneath. Sheepdogs, striving to follow, sank into soft drifts and climbed back out, whimpering as they smelt the buried animals. Surprisingly, sheep could survive for several days under snow, sometimes living off their fleeces, but when rescued were very weak and needed careful feeding if they were to survive.

The first deep snowfall found us children eager to leave our footprints on its smooth, untrodden surface. In many places birds and small animals had beaten us to it, for they were early risers. Well wrapped up, we collected our crude home-made sledge and made for the slopes of Dolgarn for hours of exhilarating fun. Once, after a hard overnight frost, we made for the same slope, not appreciating the changed conditions. In dazzling sunshine we flew over the snow at an alarming rate, gathering speed as we went. Quite unable to swing the sledge round at the foot of the slope, we ploughed into the hedge, almost precipitating ourselves into the deep lane beyond. Mu, on the front, took the brunt of the impact and needed a few minutes to recover before, licking our wounds but undeterred, we sought a gentler slope and continued our fun till dusk gathered and the crescent moon shone through the bare branches of the elms by the pool. Soft lamplight came from the kitchen window. We stamped the snow from our boots and brushed it from out coats and gloves; our bodies glowed and tingled.

Many cold, wet, winter days had to be spent indoors, with the accompanying restraint and loss of freedom. Mornings were especially irksome, for in a work-a-day room, with Mother bustling about, no peaceful corner could be found. One was hardly settled before it was time to stack the chairs on the table for the floor to be sprinkled with used tea-leaves to lay the dust preparatory to sweeping it. Perhaps the floor had to be scrubbed, the grate blackleaded, or some other disturbing job undertaken. Worst of all were washing, baking or churning days, which meant an almighty upheaval.

Washing day commenced with several journeys to the well and as many to the woodpile to heat the water needed for the operation. The clothes were immersed in a large bath of hot soapy water to soak, before being vigorously rubbed on the ribbed washing-board. There were no detergents or washing powders; washing was done with a bar of yellow washing-soap which contained a proportion of soda. The white linen was transferred to the large cast-iron boiler suspended from the sway. As the clothes boiled up they had, constantly, to be pushed down with a wooden mundle to prevent the water from boiling over and sending up clouds of ash from the fire. After rinsing, the whites were finally blued by squeezing a bag of Rickett's blue into the water. They were then mangled and carried up to the line on the windy bank behind the house.

Should washing day turn out to be wet it was postponed until better weather but, if wet weather persisted, the job had to be done and the wet clothes were draped on clothes-horses around the fire, filling the place with steam and making life thoroughly uncomfortable.

Ironing was done on the kitchen table on a folded blanket covered by a folded sheet. Flat irons, heated against the bars of the grate, were tested by spitting on the face. If the iron was sufficiently hot the moisture literally jumped off. These irons had to be carefully wiped with a damp cloth to remove all smoke and smuts. Iron-holders were essential for the blistering hot handles.

Occasionally Mother filled a charcoal iron with hot embers from the fire and thin wisps of smoke rose from its chimney as she smoothed the clothes. Another deep iron had a door at the back which could be lifted and lowered, and an accompanying set of iron clets made in its own shape. A clet was heated red-hot in the fire and dropped through the door. Both these large irons had wooden handles and needed no iron-holders, but both had the disadvantage of deadening the fire, as both embers and clets had to be changed frequently. Later a tin shield was introduced into which the heated flat-irons could be clipped, so that no part came into contact with the articles being ironed. This dispensed with the need for a damp cloth and, on the whole, proved the most satisfactory system.

Churning-day also commenced with several journeys to the well, for all equipment used in buttermaking had first to be scalded. The week's cream, fermented and thick, was stirred and poured into the scalded churn and a square, cast-iron plate, girdled with rubber, was screwed down over the opening. Churning was a tiring job and Mother had to change hands from time to time to rest her tired arms. With an occasional pause to release air, the handle was turned for twenty minutes or so until the small circular glass window in one end of the churn cleared. This signified that the butter particles had separated from the buttermilk and it was time to swing the handle from side to side to gather the particles into one lump, which could soon be felt and heard bumping against the sides of the churn as the buttermilk swished and sloshed about. The liquid was then drained off by carefully releasing a large wooden peg. With the peg replaced and the cast-iron plate removed, water was poured in to wash out the remaining buttermilk. When this was drained off, the butter was taken from the churn and put in the wooden butter-trin, where it was again washed repeatedly with ice-cold water. Salt was added and worked in evenly with ribbed, wooden butter-pats before the butter was weighed into half-pound blocks, patted into shape and marked with a pattern. Each half-pound was covered with greaseproof paper and laid on a large dish ready for market. In late autumn extra salt was added to a portion of the butter each week, and this was 'put down' in a glazed earthenware steen and stored for late winter when milk was scarce.

On baking days the kitchen was stripped of all comfort. Stems of gorse and small logs were heaped in the corner by the baking oven. The circular, dome-shaped oven, lined throughout with fire-bricks, was set about a foot back inside the kitchen wall to allow room for a flue to run up between the front of the oven and the kitchen wall. All smoke, fumes and even flames from the oven were drawn up into this flue so that none reached the kitchen itself. To heat the oven a few small sprigs of dry wood were placed on the oven floor and ignited. Gradually larger and larger stems of gorse and wood were added until the oven became red-hot. As the oven emitted a fierce heat, a long-handled scraper was employed to rake out the ashes and a damp long-handled mop to wipe over the oven floor.

From a sack of flour ground at the local mill, Mother ladled the required amount into a huge bowl, making a well in the centre. The yeast, which had previously been mixed and left to work, was poured into the well and gradually mixed with the flour. The bowl was then covered and the dough allowed to rise. While this was taking place, cakes and tarts were made to share the oven with the bread.

The dough, which by now had risen to the top of the bowl, was kneaded, cut into chunks, moulded into loaves and placed far back on the oven floor with a long-handled spade known as a peel. Tins of cakes and plates of tarts were added; those that cooked quickest were put in last so that they could be easily removed when done, and the oven door was closed.

By the time the cooking ingredients had been put away, the utensils and the kitchen floor washed, an appetising smell of bread and cakes filled the kitchen. As each item was considered done it was removed with the peel. What a relief it was to see all the bread and cakes removed from the oven and the door once more closed. A colourful curtain was draped over the oven entrance and order once more restored to the kitchen.

In the weeks leading up to Christmas extra time was spent in feeding the poultry ready for the Christmas market. Of all the jobs in the farmhouse, for me feathering was the most abhorrent.

For a couple of evenings prior to feathering the men cut wooden skewers for trussing, each ending the day with a pile of shavings beside his chair. On feathering-night the place was in an upheaval. Several women came to help and, in their coarse aprons of sacking, grouped themselves around zinc baths into which the plucked feathers were put. A large table was made ready for drawing and trussing the birds, and a second for weighing and decorating them with sprigs of parsley. It was one man's unenviable job to kill the birds and keep the featherers supplied. Very soon flecks of down from ducks and geese settled everywhere. They got up our noses and into our mouths; they settled on the heads of the featherers, ageing both blondes and brunettes by the minute. Indeed, flecks of down lingered around for days. As they were disturbed in one place they took wing to another; we even found them upstairs, where they had been carried upon our clothes and hair.

The wings of the geese were cut off at the first joint and later were pressed to make first-class sweeping agents, their feathered tips ideal for getting into awkward corners. A wing was always kept in the fender for sweeping up fallen ash.

As the birds were drawn the offensive stench of entrails and warm grease filled the room. The one redeeming feature was the fun and laughter that echoed around as tales and jokes were exchanged.

The dressed poultry were stored on the cold salting stone in the dairy to await the dead market. On market day it was stacked in the cart, covered by a sheet and an early start made for Hay, where it was sold mainly to dealers from South Wales.

10. Winter and Rough Weather

As the days closed in for winter, Mother brought out the oil lamp. She filled the bowl with paraffin, trimmed the wick, polished the glass chimney and, having lit it, suspended it over the kitchen table. At first the wick was turned up only slightly, so as to warm the chimney gradually, in order to prevent it cracking or becoming clouded by smoke. The honey-coloured light lit up the centre of the kitchen but barely reached the distant corners. We sat at the table to play ludo, snakes and ladders, snap and draughts. We practised writing and sums, or crayoned pictures. Sometimes we were called upon to make spills from the weekly news-papers for lighting candles and lanterns.

In very cold weather we forsook our hobbies to join the semi-circle round the fire, toasting the fronts of our legs and faces while our backs were exposed to draughts from all quarters. As we had known no other, we accepted these conditions and, as healthy, unpampered children, barely noticed them. From time to time someone would come in from outside bringing clouds of cold air on their clothes and skin. We looked for pictures in the fire, watched the fire-light's reflection flecking the window panes and twinkling in the polished fender. From one end of the mantlepiece a bespectacled Grandma looked down from the Mazawattee tea-caddy; at the opposite end a Horniman's caddy carried the verse,

A little old lady sat under a hill,
And if she's not gone she's sitting there still.
Wouldn't it be thoughtful for you or for me
To take her a drink of Horniman's tea?

The skillet and brass candlesticks caught the flicker of leaping flames. The singing kettle hung from the chain on the sway. In the corner of the fender the goose-wing stood on its end, ready to sweep up the ash that fell from the grate. On frosty nights blue flames hissed from the coals and sap sizzled from the ends of logs. Sticks burned through and sent up a shower of sparks and crackling flames that played on the circle of faces. Outside, screeching winds lent to the hearth an added cosiness.

In those days before the advent of radio and television, silences were broken only by the human voice, the crackling flames and the ticking clock. A neighbour dropping in with news or tales of bygone days was a welcome diversion. We children loved listening to these tales but knew better than to butt into the adults' conversation. Mother's fingers were constantly busy with darning, mending or knitting socks on four clicking steel needles. As feet slowly warmed, chilblains started itching and toes and heels were rubbed and scratched for relief. Mother's remedy was a sprig of holly with which she thrashed her chilblains till the blood came, but no one else was brave enough to try this cure.

Occasionally during the evening one of us children needed to pay a visit to the privy, so the storm lantern was lit. The path to the privy was eerie by lamplight, with menacing shadows moving about, so one sister always accompanied the other. Wind ruffled the surface of the top pool as we passed; ducks quacked sleepily on their nests in the old house ingle-nook. The privy, a 'two-holer', with lids to close when not in use, provided a resting place for the companion. With the door shut, it seemed relatively cosy by lamplight, smelling faintly of stale excrement, paraffin, whitewash and newsprint from the squares of paper, threaded on string, which served as toilet-paper. On the back of the door someone had written:

To keep this place both clean and sweet—
Open the door and close the seat.

Leaving the warmth of the fireside was a wrench, especially in the early days when we had to face the long, cold trek to the far bedrooms. Stone hotwater bottles, wrapped in our nighties, were placed in the bed an hour or so before bedtime.

We shared the large bedroom with Granny. Our iron-framed, brass-knobbed bedstead stood on one side of the room, its head against the west wall, near the window. Granny's large four-poster stood on the opposite side, its head against the east wall. Between the beds, and facing the window, was a large chest-of-drawers accommodating our best clothes. One drawer was reserved for Dad's market jacket and breeches and his Sunday suit. All were thoroughly brushed and carefully folded before being put away. There were no wardrobes. At the foot of Granny's bed was the washstand and alongside it, near the window, the dressing-table. A small table stood at the head of Granny's bed for the candle and matches, while we had to make do with a bedside chair. In the centre of the room was a large armchair commode. Over the chest-of-drawers a framed, embroidered text said: 'God is Love', and a second, over the head of our bed: 'Suffer little children'. There was no carpet on the stained floor-boards—just rugs beside the beds.

At bedtime the brass warming-pan was filled with glowing embers from the fire, and with one hand cupped around the candle Mother led the bedtime procession. Dad followed with the warming-pan, leaving Mu and me to bring up the rear. Up the steps from the kitchen we went, along the first passage, through the sitting room, along the second passage, through a door into the small hall at the foot of the far staircase, and so upstairs. As each door was opened *en route,* strong draughts threatened to extinguish the candle, despite Mother's sheltering hand. Fumes wafted back from the warming-pan, to sting our noses and throats. We held hands and kept close to Dad, for the feeble light of the guttering candle lit only the path immediately ahead, and who could say what ogres lurked in the darkness on either side or crept up in the blackness behind? Alongside the foot of the staircase the cellar steps led down into the yawning blackness, affording concealment for who could say what? We dared not glance over our shoulders as we climbed the stairs, for fear of enticing some demon to follow.

In the bedroom a second candle was lit for Mother, who stayed to put the warming pan between the sheets, listen to our prayers and settle us into bed. In the darkness we cootched up together and were soon as warm as toast. With knees tucked up, one sat in the other's lap; when one turned, the other followed. Soon fast asleep, we slept till morning, while on cold nights Jack Frost crept in to paint the window-panes with silver leaves and ferns, completely obscuring the outside view. On exceptionally cold nights his long icy fingers reached the ewer and the chamber-pots under the bed.

In times of sickness an oil-stove brought a comforting rosy glow to the bedroom, throwing a pretty, rose-patterned light on the ceiling. Care had to be taken to place it away from draughts, which encouraged the flame to draw up and emit smoky fumes and greasy black smuts that covered everything in the room.

*　　*　　*　　*

As Christmas drew near we settled down to write and address our Christmas cards, ready for posting on December 24th. None were ever posted earlier and all safely reached their destinations on Christmas Day.

Our postwoman lived far up in the hills and had a four mile journey on horse-back or bicycle to collect the mail before commencing her eleven-mile round. For this she was paid seventeen shillings a week. Whatever the weather she never failed to bring the mail except when roads were blocked by snow; she also brought all manner of news collected on her rounds.

One local postwoman's round took her over a hill, and though she travelled this route daily and knew the hill like the back of her hand, one day in thick fog she found herself going round in circles, returning again and again to the same place. After several attempts she gave up the struggle and jocularly yelled, ''Oman lost! 'Oman lost! And a *good* 'oman, too!'

On Christmas Eve the kitchen was decked with holly and mistletoe. In the corner by the baking oven, small candles fixed to the Christmas tree lit up the tinsel and decorations to give the room a festive air. We loved this unaccustomed, convivial atmosphere, but as small children we were always ready for bed early, fearing Santa Claus would arrive before we were asleep and leave no presents. Feigning sleep, we were told, would be useless, for he'd know at once. Mother tied our socks to the bed-posts and advised us to try to get to sleep quickly. We slept lightly at first, subconsciously alert for the visitor, drowsily awakening from time to time to see Mother hovering around with the candle. Finally, dead tired, we sank into deep sleep, neither hearing the sleighbells outside nor Santa tiptoeing in with the presents.

We woke long before daylight, our thoughts flying at once to the stockings on the bed-posts. Groping around in the darkness we found them bulging with gifts. Hurrah! He had been! In the dark we tried to guess the contents: both had similar things. There was something round, something soft—when would daylight come? At first light each found perhaps an apple, an orange, a sugar mouse, a packet of sweets, a hankie. Later, beside the bed, we discovered larger presents—perhaps a Noah's ark, a box of jig-saw bricks, a game, a pencil box. We could hardly wait to be called to get up.

During the morning the postwoman arrived with a huge pile of mail. Several envelopes were actually addressed to us personally. What a thrill it was to discover the senders!

Each year parties of carol singers crept up to the door and startled us with a burst of song. Usually they disguised themselves by blackening their faces and wearing false beards and moustaches, and we had great fun discovering their identities.

New Year's gifting had more or less died out by the time we were old enough to go far on our own, but Mother taught us the old rhyme and sent us to our nearest neighbours—the Owens of Ty'n-y-cwm. Outside their door we chanted the old rhyme:

New Year's gift! New Year's gift!
We wish you a Merry Christmas
And a Happy New Year,
A pocket full of money and a cellar full of beer,
A good fat pig to last you all the year.
So please give us a New Year's gift, this new year.
The roads are very dirty, our boots are very thin,
We have a little pocket to pop a penny in.
The cock was in the roosting-house, the hen came chuckling by,
Please give us a penny, or a mince-pie.
If you haven't a penny, a ha'penny will do,
If you haven't a ha'penny, God bless you.
New Year's gift! New Year's gift!
Please give us a New Year's gift, this new year.

* * * *

On wild, wet, windy nights, when the sycamore on the bank outside our window groaned and creaked eerily and rain lashed the window panes, we snuggled down deeper into our feathered nest and pulled the blankets over our ears.

Occasionally, on bright moonlit nights, we heard the weird bark of a vixen as she answered her mate, and imagined her stealing along the shadow of the hedgerow towards the fowlhouse beyond the tree. Such a cackling and squawking, we knew, would greet her arrival. Should she find a loose board or small hole she'd soon be inside, causing immense havoc by killing fowl after fowl just for the fun of it before finally leaving with one or two.

Usually we sank into deep sleep from which we never woke till morning, but one summer's night I woke to deep silence: not a sound was to be heard inside or out. For a while I lay listening, then panic seized me. I knew, beyond doubt, that everyone had gone away and forsaken us. I shot out of bed, flew downstairs and burst breathless into the kitchen, only to find my parents chatting with friends. How utterly foolish I felt! Ashamed to admit my fears, I buried my scarlet cheeks in Mother's lap before being escorted, shamefaced back to bed.

On summer nights, when no candle was needed to light the way, we were sent to bed alone. As the sun still shone outside it seemed too early for sleep. We made nests and tents with the bed-clothes. Too far from the kitchen to be heard, we chased each other round the room. Up over the footrail of the bed we went, scattering the brass bed-knobs in our wake till, finally exhausted, we fell asleep.

One night Mu hurt her foot in the rough-and-tumble. For days it remained swollen and painful, so Mother took her in the trap to Mrs. Drew, the bonesetter, who lived some eight miles away. Mrs. Drew came from a long line of bonesetters who had lived in the area for many years. Generations of folks from far and near had sought relief from the family and few had left disappointed. Chatting to Mu, Mrs. Drew gently took the injured foot, felt it all over, then suddenly gave it a sharp wrench; there was a click, a gasp from Mu, and the pain was gone.

We were delighted when the new bedrooms were completed. In the new surroundings we felt for a time as though we were on holiday. By now we were allowed our own candle to light ourselves to bed. Occasionally the carrier got a shock from hot grease spilt on her hand when she neglected to hold the candlestick upright. No longer isolated from the family, we douted the candle and drifted into sleep to the smell of hot candle-grease and smoking wick, to men's voices in the yard and murmurs of conversation from the kitchen, giving us a nice cosy feeling of security.

Our bedroom window overlooked the farmyard and faced the Little Mountain. Each morning our eyes strayed to the lonely thorn tree on the mountain's brow. This little tree played an important part in our lives. It was used regularly to point out the position of a sheep or pony or for directing in some other way. Little did we guess that this small tree carried on its trunk a 'goodbye cross' cut by the diarist, the Rev. Francis Kilvert, before he left the district, a fact he had recorded in his diary more than fifty years before. Had we known of its existence, what fun we would have had searching for it and also for the other crosses he had cut on trees near Caeau Farm, which we often passed on errands to Crowther's Pool and other places.

11. School Days

Newchurch School was opened in 1880 and, according to the old Log Book, no child admitted on that opening day or in the ensuing months could either read or write. Prior to this a small school had been kept in the Newchurch Rectory by the Rev. David Vaughan or his curate, catering, it would seem, for the favoured few. Vaughan, a farmer as well as a rector, lived with his large family at a farm called Gilfach-yr-hoel, not far from the village, leaving the mainly vacant Rectory with ample accommodation for a small school.

It was to this Rectory School that Francis Kilvert, the famous diarist, walked 'ten miles for a kiss', and 'fluttered the dove-cot not a little' by arriving unexpectedly and finding 'sweet Emmeline' bravely keeping school while the curate was away. For having done five sums he rewarded Janet with a kiss. This was in May 1870.

The new school was not built in the village but a mile distant on the Glascwm road, a site presumably chosen as the most central position for the catchment area, which at that time took in children from parts of Glascwm and Colva as well. The Rev. Vaughan took a keen interest in the new school and visited it almost daily during term time for nearly twenty years.

Because of its close proximity to Cwmgwilym Farm the school was known, locally, as Cwmgwilym School. With a house attached, it stood on the corner of the lane leading to the farm. A wall surmounted by iron railings ran along the front of the house and school and continued round the corner of the lane to the boys' playground. The grass-covered area within these railings was known as the green yard and was used only on fine summer days. Two iron gates gave access to flights of steps and gravelled paths, one leading to the school-house and the other to the front door of the school. This door was rarely used, the usual entrance being by a back door opening off the boys' playground. A high wall, with wide, corrugated iron doors at one end, divided the boys' playground from the girls' small yard, which was tucked away behind the school. These doors allowed access to the coal-shed, which stood alongside the primitive toilets in the girls' playground.

The stone-built school had but one large classroom, inadequately heated by two slow-combustion Tortoise stoves. High windows denied the picturesque surroundings to those seated in their iron-framed, ink-bespattered desks, and revealed nothing but sky. High in one gable-end was the school bell, its tolling-rope dangling beside the classroom wall.

The stone-built lean-to cloakroom or porch, as we termed it, had two windows side by side beneath which were four wash-basins, each with a cold-water tap. Behind each of the two outside doors a roller-towel was fixed, one for the boys and one for the girls. Row of pegs ran round the walls, those at the front for the girls, the rest for the boys.

The caretaker lived with her large family in a cottage on a steep hillside almost a mile from the school. In those days caretakers were expected to provide both kindling wood and cleaning materials. For their work they received a mere pittance. The caretaker gathered her wood where she could, and on wet days experienced great difficulty in getting her fires started. A second journey had to be made in the late afternoon, to clean and sweep, before again climbing the steep hill to her cottage. We often met her in her rusty black coat and hat and well-worn, soil-stained boots, returning from her morning duties or arriving for afternoon cleaning. Little wonder that she looked thin and haggard.

At the time of our admission the school had but one teacher, responsible for the education of twenty-five to thirty pupils ranging in age from five to fourteen years. With so few books and so little equipment provided, this was a daunting task. In fact, trying to keep so many age-groups fully and interestingly occupied proved impossible and resulted in disciplinary problems. The older boys were completely out of control and got up to all kinds of mischief. They took great delight in removing the hair-pins from the bun at the back of the teacher's head, allowing her hair to fall over her shoulders, and constantly teased her about a local man whom, they said, she secretly admired. She spent a great deal of time reading stories which, no doubt, proved an excellent way of keeping unruly pupils interested and the whole school under her eye. Basic subjects were badly neglected.

In those days teachers dreaded an inspector's visit, for he invariably came to censure and criticise. A poor report meant, at best, severe criticism, at worst, dismissal. When, in 1926, word reached the school of an impending visit, it was obvious to us all that the teacher was worried and her anxiety was transmitted to us. Every step to school, on that dreaded morning, was a reluctant one; our very hearts quailed within us.

All morning neither teacher nor pupils could concentrate on the work in hand; all ears were strained for the arrival of the visitor. When the vehicle was eventually heard to draw up and the handle of the porch door to turn, hearts thumped and fear drained the colour from several faces.

The classroom door opened to admit a tall, stern-looking man with a condescending expression which did nothing to calm our fears. A couple of infants, overwhelmed by tense atmosphere, burst into tears.

Exercises were set before us; the inspector sauntered up and down the aisles. Tense and frightened, we were quite incapable of giving our best, poor though it was. When he hovered over a child's desk his very presence scattered the few thoughts the child had collected, rendering him incapable of putting pen to paper until the presence had moved on. Oral questions were even worse; his voice and manner numbed our brains. Even when we felt we knew the answer we were afraid to voice it, lest it should be wrong and bring wrath and sarcasm down on our heads.

The relief when he finally left was almost tangible. For a minute, silence reigned, then our relieved teacher dismissed us. In the playground we all chattered at once, discussing the recent ordeal before laughing and shouting for joy that the nightmare was over.

All this was brought back vividly to my mind many years later, when I listened to an inspector relating *his* early experiences. He related how he had arrived at a school one day, unexpectedly, and had introduced himself to the elderly headmistress. The words 'His Majesty's Inspector', so dreaded over the years, brought an expression of horror to her face and she fell at his feet in a dead faint. Several minutes later a young assistant entering the room was astounded to find a strange man on his knees, cradling the headmistress's head in his lap, trying to force cold water through her pallid lips to restore her to consciousness.

Another story described how, in a place where two schools were but a short distance apart, each headmaster had apparently agreed to notify the other immediately an inspector's vehicle drew up outside his school. When, one morning, he drew up outside School A, the headmaster, true to his word, had scribbled a note and despatched a boy hotfoot with it to School B. Unfortunately the inspector had popped in only to appraise the head of his intention of calling on him later in the day, after first examining School B. The inspector had travelled but a short distance in the direction of the second school when he overtook a lad in the lane and stopped to offer him a lift. Finding the lad was bound for the same school as himself, with a note for the headmaster, he offered to deliver the note and save the boy the journey. After some hesitation the note was handed over, and on it the inspector read: 'The devil has just pulled up outside, so expect him this afternoon.' What must have been the headmaster's reaction on the boy's return, knowing he would have to face 'the devil' later in the day?

Newchurch School group (author third from right in front row. Mu immediately behind).

In 1926 an infant-teacher was appointed to Newchurch School, and the following year the headmistress resigned and a new headmistress was appointed. These changes, possibly due to a poor inspector's report, heralded a better era for the school. The new headmistress was strict; troublemakers dared not try their tricks on her. How sadly we all lamented the former, easy-going days.

Utterly appalled at our ignorance, the new headmistress set about the formidable task of bringing the work up to a reasonable standard. Each morning, time was allotted for table-testing and mental arithmetic. As with all repetitive work I found table-learning easy but I dreaded mental arithmetic, and someone else's hand usually shot up before I was confident enough to commit myself. In arithmetic every other sum was marked with a red cross, and one glance at our English books brought from the headmistress the exclamation 'Och!' Reading lessons tried her patience to the extreme, the words often having to be dragged out of the readers. The hours I had spent in the old house teaching my imaginary class to read stood me in good stead and helped to give me the confidence I normally lacked.

So much time was given to catching up on the three R's that little was left for other studies. Geography lessons consisted mainly of learning the names of seas and oceans, bays and headlands. We chanted them like tables: 'Flamborough Head, Spurn Head, Lowestoft Ness, The Naze,— North Foreland, South Foreland, Dungeness, Beachy Head, Selsey Bill'. We picked out the various countries and continents from the world map and were proud to learn that all the red patches were parts of the great British Empire, on which the sun never set. History lessons consisted of stories of well-known historical characters and events. We were never enlightened as to the sequence of the various dynasties. As a result they have always puzzled me and, as for dates, I could never remember them anyway.

Much attention was given to handwriting. In copy-books we copied, in 'thin up, thick down' cursive writing, proverbs such as 'A still tongue makes a wise head' and 'Spare the rod and spoil the child'.

Once a week, while the boys had a drawing lesson, we girls had to endure a lesson in needlework. We started by making a hem on unbleached calico which was almost too tough to force the needle through. The result was uneven stitches that had to be taken out repeatedly. Long before we had reached the end of the hem the stitches were black, the material a dirty grey and the whole hem spotted with blood from our pricked fingers. We progressed to making petticoats and pinafores in cotton or winceyette but no really pretty material or thread ever came our way.

Occasionally boys, as well as girls, were given sewing-cards to work with coloured cotton. These we enjoyed. Each card had the outline of a flower, bird or geometric pattern stamped on it, with dots at equal distances along the outline. We placed the card on a felt pad and with an awl-like instrument pierced the dots, then back-stitched from hole to hole to complete the picture.

The infants' class, under its new teacher, was provided with slates and pencils with which to practise forming letters and figures. The slates were rubbed clean with rags (on which the children were often obliged to spit) in order to remove all previous marks. They were promoted to small books and lead pencils and, eventually, amongst blots and smudges, to pen and ink. All books and equipment were in very short supply; every scrap of paper had to be used. Pencils were discarded only when too short to hold, new nibs given only when writing with the old ones became impossible. Each ink-user was provided with a small piece of blotting paper which had to last for weeks. Nothing was ever wasted.

Nowadays, when children commence school, the teacher often has difficulty in persuading them to refrain from chattering. During our early childhood the teacher had an uphill job getting a single word out of some newcomers. For days they sat too shy to speak. In the heart of the country small children saw few people outside their own families. When a visitor called they buried their faces in their mother's skirts and allowed her to answer for them. Starting school was a traumatic experience for such children. Leaving the familiar atmosphere of home, they were plunged into strange surroundings, amongst strange faces, and expected to answer questions with no mother at hand to help. It took weeks for some to summon the courage to answer a question, and months to find the nerve to ask one. Many were far too shy to ask to 'leave the room', occasionally with disastrous results. When a peripatetic master took charge for a while and one child plucked up courage to ask, 'Please, sir, may I leave the room?' his reply, to her utter bewilderment, was, 'Aye, don't take it with you.'

A conscientious man, this teacher slogged hard to improve the standard of work but found the going tough. One day, after explaining a certain point over and over again without success, he groaned, 'I might as well talk to my grandmother, and she's been dead fifty years.' Then, in sheer frustration, he changed classes with the infants' teacher, arriving to find her explaining the meaning of the word 'horizon'. Taking over from there he said, 'Now, children, you see the sky over there through the window; it looks as if it's touching the ground, doesn't it? Well, we call that skyline the horizon. What do we call it, children?' There was no reply. He tried again. 'The skyline, children, where the sky appears to meet the ground, we call that the horizon. What do we call it?' Still there was no answer; all were far too scared to say a word. Utterly exasperated, he yelled, 'Well, we call it the blinking horizon! Now what do we call it?' 'The blinking horizon, sir,' piped up a timid voice. Disgusted, he turned tail and returned to his own class.

So remote was the school that we had few callers in those motorless days. One regular visitor was the district nurse, who came mainly for what were known as cleanliness inspections. This chiefly involved examining heads, for head-lice were a problem in those days. The children of one or two families were regularly found to have dirty heads, putting the whole school at risk. Mu and I had only to scratch our heads for Mother to descend on us with a small-tooth nit comb. We fretted and fumed as we suffered the operation, repeatedly yelling, 'Oh, it's pugging!' as the fine comb found the tangles in our hair. But being a sparsely populated district we had few of the usual childish epidemics such as measles, mumps and chicken-pox which many, no doubt, suffered with greater discomfort in adult life.

Another regular visitor was the attendance officer, for children, especially boys, were frequently kept at home to help on the farm. His cruel sarcastic tongue lashed these unfortunate offenders, though the fault lay not with them but with their parents. Some farmers had little time for education, arguing that boys who were destined to spend their lives on a farm were better employed learning farming skills.

Whatever the season we could scarcely wait for playtime and some food from our satchels, for the morning walk to school gave us healthy appetites. Our sandwiches were made from wholemeal bread baked in the farmhouse oven. How we envied the village children their nice white boughten bread! On very wet or cold days we ate our lunch indoors, seated around the classroom stoves, where some children toasted their cheese on steel knitting needles. We played indoor games such as Blind Man's Buff and Hunt the Thimble.

In dry weather each sex kept to its respective playground. The boys seemed to play nothing but football. When we heard the ball strike the corrugated iron doors separating the playgrounds we knew a goal had been scored. The gateway into the lane served as a second goal.

The girls had a choice of several games. A great favourite was Jackie Lantern. For this game all but two of the players became sheep and formed a circle, holding hands. Of the remaining two, one became the owner of the sheep, taking up her position in the centre of the ring, while the other became Jackie Lantern and circled the ring. The dialogue ran thus:

Owner: Who goes round my garden wall this time of night?

Jackie: Only little Jackie Lantern.

Owner: Don't you steal one of my fat sheep!

Jackie: Only one tonight and one tomorrow night. Come along with me, little Jackie Lantern.'

Here Jackie tapped a sheep on the back and it left the ring to attach itself behind him. The game continued until all the sheep had been taken from the ring and formed a long tail behind Jackie. The owner had then to recapture her flock one by one by touching the one on the end of the tail and growing a tail herself with the captives till she had regained all her sheep.

Singing games were very popular, enjoyed as much for the singing as for the game. One catchy tune we enjoyed singing was:

The wind, the wind, the wind blows high,
The rain comes scattering from the sky.
She is handsome, she is pretty,
She is the fairest of the city;
Catch her by her lilywhite hand
And lead her over the water;
Give her kisses one, two, three,
For she's Mrs (Somebody's) daughter.

There was no room in our small playground for individual skipping-ropes, even had we been fortunate enough to possess them, but we spent much time skipping with a long rope, with a girl at either end turning. We usually chose games that had an accompanying rhyme, such as this:

Lady, lady, touch the ground,
Lady, lady, turn around.
Lady, lady, show your toe,
Lady, lady, out you go!

Or, for two children together:

Every morning at eight o'clock
You will hear the postman knock.
Postman, postman, drop your letter;
Lady, lady, pick it up.

On sunny summer playtimes we were allowed in the green yard, where we lazed on the grass or played leapfrog, high jump or long jump, taking advantage of a soft grassy landing. During summer dinner-hours we wandered through sunny buttercup fields down to the River Arrow, at this point not far from its source. Evidence of winter floods could still be seen where the high water had left debris in the lower branches of the alders and in the hedges beside the river. We sat on the banks to make daisy chains or stripped their petals to forecast our matrimonial futures, while the shallow, sunlit water winked and tinkled over the stones and the deep, dark stretches, near the bank, glided noislessly by, reflecting in their depths the overhanging branches with glimpses of blue sky between. Once in a while we spotted a trout gliding to the shelter of a large stone or deep hole under the bank, or spied a beautiful dragon-fly with bright blue gauzy wings, dancing above the water. The air was fresh and sweet with the smell of the river and the scent of the alder and willow. On very hot days the banks were strewn with our pollen-covered shoes and socks while we paddled in the water searching for bullyheads and lifting large stones to see what hid beneath. We emerged with legs and feet pink from the chilly water. Too soon the happy hour had flown; the school bell called us back to a sombre, dreary classroom.

I shall never forget one dinner-hour when we visited a different stretch of the river. Here, the current had cut into the nearside bank so that it overhung the water. By taking a run we could jump the river to land on flat shingle on the far side. That day we were heading for a copse on the opposite slope. Unfortunately, I had sprained my ankle and was unable to jump. Determined I should not be left behind, the boys piled large stones in the water and carefully lowered me down. Alas! under my weight, the stones slipped, landing me in deep water where I was drenched to the skin. A gallant boy called Tom jumped in and hauled me out. The copse was forgotten as sticks were hastily gathered to kindle a fire. Willing hands held my outer garments to the flames while I stood near to dry my underwear, but before I was half dry we heard the tolling bell and I had to dress in a hurry. We scurried back to school via a footbridge some distance away and earned a downright scolding for arriving late. When the teacher's eye fell on me and discovered the reason for my sad plight we were scolded again for 'crass stupidity'. I was removed to the schoolhouse, divested of my wet clothes and attired in garments from the head teacher's wardrobe. As she was a tall person and I a short, ten year old, the fit left much to be desired and when I returned to class my friends were hard put to it to restrain their mirth. My own clothes were pegged to the schoolhouse clothes-line and by home-time were dry enough to wear.

On the whole the children got on well together and few quarrels broke out. But boys were fond of picking on one or two poor girls from large families as they passed through their playground *en route* for the cloakroom. They pulled their hair, tripped them up and molested them generally. A gang would fall on one of these unfortunates and shove her up into a corner; then all would line up and push as hard as they could. The poor girl would yell, 'I'm dying, I'm dying,' but no heed would be paid to her cries. Some girls joined in these attacks, callously enjoying the fun; others, like myself, were on tenterhooks till the victim was released, fearing she really would be crushed to death.

In those days children from poor families were shabbily dressed in patched, ill-fitting clothes handed down from older brothers and sisters, and in broken, down-at-heel boots. In our early days at the school most, if not all, girls wore pinafores over their dresses and hats held on with elastic under the chins. Older boys wore corduroy breeches and stout hobnailed boots with steel tips on toes and heels. All boys wore short trousers and socks in summer; in winter the younger boys wore knee-length trousers and long socks or stockings that covered the knees.

Many children, but more especially boys, spoke only in dialect. To have done otherwise would have laid themselves open to accusations of being 'stuck up' or of 'trying to make theirselves out to be somebody'. When addressing the teacher they struggled to use the King's English, but were seldom grammatically correct.

12. School Journeys

We had the choice of two routes to school: 'over the hill' or 'round the road'.

On wet days, clad in coats topped by hooded capes and shod in stout, sprigged boots, we took the unpopular route 'round the road', via the village. On either side hedges hung with crystal raindrops and sheets of rain swept the valley sides. With both coats and capes our bodies were fairly well protected but our legs were exposed to the storm and to water dripping from our capes. Long before we reached school our socks were saturated and water trickled down into our boots, soaking our feet and chaffing our legs where the hard boot-tops rubbed them. We arrived dripping, bedraggled and wretched.

I cannot recall any attempt being made to dry our clothes. Probably, with all pupils arriving in a similar condition, it was well nigh impossible. We just sat and dried out as the day progressed. At home-time we had the discomfort of donning wet coats—small wonder the journey 'round the road' was so unpopular. We hated the stout boots too and greatly envied town children their lighter, daintier footwear. I well remember my first pair of shiny, black, fleecy-lined Wellington boots, so soft and light when compared with the leather ones that I felt I was walking on air.

Whenever possible we took the narrow, winding path up through the gorse bushes above the well for the journey 'over the hill'. On spring mornings the air smelt of rising sap and bursting buds. Fleecy clouds alternately captured and released the sun, and spiders' webs on every bush sparkled with crystal dewdrops. Water oozed from the turf with every step and rabbits threw up sprays of moisture behind them as they ran in all directions.

Curlews welcomed the spring with their bubbling trills, lapwings wheeled and tumbled in joy. We listened each day for the first cuckoo and imitated its call to deceive our friends. Soon swallows and martins arrived to skim the ponds, and swifts to scythe through the sky. At the mountain pool we collected frogspawn to take with us, for no school was without its frogspawn in spring. Indeed, in his essay on spring, one child wrote, 'In spring sheep have lambs, hens have chickens and teachers have tadpoles!'

Best of all were the lovely, lovely days of early summer when scented bracken fronds unfurled to edge our velvet path; when larks carolled overhead and mountain pansies bloomed at our feet. Lightly clad and shod, we skipped blithely along, pausing each morning to wash away our freckles in the pearly dew. On those heavenly mornings our hearts overflowed with joy in our beautiful surroundings. We could scarcely bear the ecstasy and often retraced our steps to tread the enchanted way again.

Alone on one such day I decided, on impulse, to spend it on the hill. The morning was superb, with larks rising in the sunshine and small white clouds sailing in the sky. Feeling free as the creatures around me, I ran up and down the velvet paths through the bracken and basked in the sunshine on soft green turf, watching the cotton-wool clouds gradually thinning out and disappearing into the blue. The air was full of song and of small noises and stirrings as nature's lesser creatures went about their daily tasks. How much better was this than confinement in a classroom!

But a whole school day is a long time for a small child to spend alone. After a couple of hours I doubted that my idea had been such a good one. What else could I do? I was tired of running up the paths and lying in the sun. It was too late to go on, too soon to go back. Suddenly, an alarming thought flashed through my mind: 'How should I know when it was time to start for home?' If I arrived back at a ridiculous hour my sins would be found out. I anxiously scanned the surroundings for some indication of time but found none. Another problem presented itself: suppose someone working in a field on the opposite slope spotted me. I hurried down to the hedge for concealment and spent the rest of the time there, trying to decide when to start for home. Eventually I set out in trepidation, pausing at the corner of the lane above the well for a final attempt to find some clue to the time. Again I found none. There was nothing for it but to venture forth and take the consequence. When no comment was voiced on my arrival, I could scarcely believe my luck and vowed never to put myself in such a risky position again. I cannot recall what excuse I offered to the mistress the following day for my absence but no one ever knew I had spent all that day on the hill.

On fine autumn mornings, when sun shone through thin mists, softening the outlines of banks and trees, the peace of the hillside was broken by the fern-cutters' scythes ripping through the hard stems and filling the air with the scent of bruised fern.

Late autumn days held a hint of sadness. Dank and dying fronds fell across our path. Fields and hillsides slowly lost their colour and the sun its warmth. All too soon we would wake to a sting at the back of our noses and find Jack Frost had returned. Sounds were sharp and clear. From our bedroom we heard the purr of the bellows as the fire was coaxed to burn; the clatter of crockery and cutlery as the breakfast table was laid; the ring of men's boots on the frozen fold. Never too eager to rise, it was torture to do so on these cold mornings and we had to be called several times before we consented to leave our cosy bed. Shivering, we dressed quickly and rushed to the comparative warmth of the kitchen to wash.

Winter came bleak and cold to the hillside. The rock-hard path, through frosted bracken, rang to our every step. Amongst the sere bushes the little pool was a sheet of rippled ice. Biting winds whistled through frost-webbed hedges. With hands and feet numbed by cold we were glad to reach the school porch and feel the tingling glow that the cold air had imparted to our bodies. When cold weather persisted, the ink in our wells froze and, except for the fortunate few who sat near the stove, all feet would ache with cold by playtime. There is little wonder we all suffered from chilblains. On those dark days leading up to Christmas we started for school before it was fully light and returned as night was closing in.

Then came the morning, usually early in the new year, when we woke to an ultra-white ceiling, a lighter-than-usual room, and silence. Outside a white carpet muffled all steps. Feathery flakes were falling from a leaden sky. School was out of the question, for heavy snow soon filled the narrow roads to the hedge-tops. Then men from every farm and cottage turned out with shovels to dig a pathway through—a job that might have to be repeated more than once as strong winds blew the piled-up snow back into the cleared paths. These narrow tracks, between high walls of snow, were our only links with the outside world. If persistent hard frosts followed a heavy snowfall we were able to walk from place to place over buried gates and hedges. When conditions allowed a return to school it inevitably meant subjection to cold and, sometimes, hard snowballs, which stung the skin and trickled icily down the neck. How I loathed snowballs!

Our morning journeys over the hill were usually uneventful, but one morning the peace of the hillside was shattered by a piercing, terrified cry. There, beside our path, was a tiny rabbit caught in a snare and a stoat disappearing into the bracken, thwarted of its intended carnage by our approach. The rabbit, hypnotised by fear till the stoat had vanished, came to life, plunging hither and thither in a frantic attempt to escape but succeeding only in tightening the cruel noose around its neck. Our tender hearts ached and we resolved to set it free. ''Old on to 'is ears,' command-ed Mu, 'while I loosen the wire.' With the terrified rabbit leaping and plunging about that was easier said than done. After many attempts we succeeded in freeing it, only to hear the distant tolling bell. We took to our heels and ran for life, but the school was over half a mile away and we had little chance of arriving in time. Puffing and panting, we tried to think of a convincing excuse to offer, till, thoroughly out of breath, we could run no more. Our arrival at school was met by an ominous silence which meant that prayers were over. Oh dear, what would the teacher say? Mu slowly and carefully turned the iron ring in the porch door, trying to lift the latch quietly but, as usual, it gave a loud click that coud be heard by all inside. Biting our lower lips we looked anxiously at each other, knowing there was now no escape from the scolding in store. We entered sheepishly and stood before the teacher's desk, conscious that all eyes were upon us and everyone agog to hear what would be said. Having found no convincing excuse there was nothing for it but to tell the truth. As our story unfolded we noticed the teacher's angry expression change to one of interest. To our great surprise she commended us on our kindly deed. No more was said about our late arrival and we went thankfully to our seats, stunned by this unexpected turn of events, leaving the class somewhat disappointed.

Always reluctant to leave the hill path for the dull, prosaic road, muddy in winter and dusty in summer, we skipped down the steep intervening fields, scanning the opposite pastures for our friends Gladys and Gwen, who lived on the opposite side of the valley. Sometimes we spotted them waving from the bank beside the pine wood and all ran to meet at the facing roadside gates. When they were nowhere to be seen we examined the gatepost for the stone they would have left if they had already gone by. If we found no stone we left one on the gatepost ourselves to let them know we were ahead.

The homeward journey was shared, for the first half-mile or so, with schoolmates. In the early days, when Gladys and Gwen's brother John and his friend Elwyn were still in school, they carried us, in turn, on their backs to shorten the journey. When they had left school the road seemed endless.

We enlivened the way by swinging on a new, creosoted gate, which we called the black gate. Time and again we hauled it open for the short ride back to the post, quite aware that this meant trouble if we were caught, but there was never anyone near to censure or to see. No other gate, on our route, could provide a ride to compare with that on the black gate.

In summer, Kathleen, the blacksmith's daughter, brought ginger-beer to school to drink. The rest of us, with our bottles of cold, milky tea or Camp coffee, envied her this and someone, probably Mu, persuaded her to keep the beer each day for home-time, so that we could play 'taking communion' on the way home. Near the black gate we sat on the verge for

Mu, Gladys and Gwen (left to right), author seated.

the service, quaffed deeply when offered 'the wine', and brought the refreshing service to a close when the bottle was empty.

When the only house on our route became vacant, we turned aside to see what new diversion this could offer. Racing down the short lane to it, we made straight for the front door but were disappointed to find it locked. Fearing someone might spot us from the road, we headed for seclusion round the back. Where the bank reached almost to the eaves, we found a tiny, two-paned window unlatched. This whetted our appetites for an interior inspection and, after a brief discussion, I, the youngest and smallest, was shoved in head-first. Noticing there was a huge drop to the floor I gesticulated frantically and was withdrawn to be fed in feet-first to land the right way up. Once inside I admitted the accomplices by the front door. What we expected to find in an empty house is anyone's guess. Eagerly we raced from room to room, our footsteps echoing in the emptiness. We found nothing and left, disillusioned, by the front door, which had to remain unlocked.

A favourite pastime on the homeward journey was making birds' nests in the hedge-banks, or ditches, as we oddly called them. We collected suitable materials and took great pains in constructing realistic-looking nests, angling for each other's compliments with: 'Come and look at mine.'

In spring we searched for real nests and few, however well concealed, escaped our sharp eyes. Best of all we liked the robin's nest, tucked so neatly and cleverly in a niche in the bank. Some were so well concealed that had not the sitting birds panicked as we hovered near, even our sharp eyes would have missed them. Each, in turn, carefully put in her hand to touch the tiny eggs, hot from the mother's breast. Another favourite was the soft, mossy, hair-lined nest of the chaffinch. Whatever the nest, its whereabouts was kept secret from the big boys, who would have blown the eggs to add to their collections.

As we ambled along we searched the wayside hedges for something to eat. We ate the juicy sweet-briar and the leaves and flowers of the wood-sorrel, which we called cuckoos' bread and cheese. We ate hawthorn leaves and berries and the leaves of the sorrel, which we named sour leaves. We threaded wild strawberries on long bents and sat down to a feast when several bents were full. In autumn there were nuts and blackberries, wild raspberries and plums to feast on. Sometimes we chose a small swede from a field and peeled it, dirt and all, with our teeth.

Periodically we came upon the roadman breaking stones with his long-handled stone-hammer to fill the many potholes in the unsurfaced roads.

He was solely responsible for the upkeep of several miles, and before he could finish one stretch another was crying out for attention. His was a long day, culminating in a long tramp back to his small cottage by the stream. Many were the days when he must have returned home wet to the skin despite the protection of the thick sack he wore over his shoulders. No allowance was made for bad weather: if he didn't work he wasn't paid. His calloused hands, almost as hard as the handle of his hammer, were often chapped and, in cold weather, broken from chilblains.

As he espied us approaching he usually took out his large pocket-watch, in its celluloid case, to check the time, before hailing us, always with the same words, 'Here they come Darby and Joan, Jenny Lind and Blaencerdi Bob.' We always stopped for a chat. His piles of stones, dotted here and there along the verge, made capital mounds on which to play King of the Castle, and were left considerably flattened when the game was over. Somewhere along the route we came upon his wheelbarrow and used it to give each other rides, thoughtlessly abandoning it wherever we happened to be when we tired of the game. Once he came to see Dad to complain about this, pointing Mu out as the ringleader. Then, probably not wishing to sound too censorious, he added, 'But this other is the best gel in Radnorshire.'

For some reason at that time it was common to see children's hands covered with warts. Most children had a few. We anointed them with the white, creamy sap of the spurge we found growing in the banks, mainly, I think, because it looked like ointment. Mu, whose hands were covered with warts, was advised by a local 'conjurer' to rub them all over with a black slug, before impaling it on a thorn bush. When the slug shrivelled the warts would shrivel too. Another suggested she count her warts carefully, put the same number of rice grains in a packet and leave it at a cross-roads. Whoever picked it up would inherit the warts and leave her free of them. As far as I know she did neither of these things. Her warts disappeared as suddenly as they had come.

Each morning, before starting for school, we were charged to 'Mind to come straight home and not loiter.' But occasionally the tug of friendship proved too strong and instead of parting company at the facing gates we took the longer route together 'round the road'. Reaching the brow of the road, overlooking the village, we sometimes heard, in the silence of those traffic-free days, the distant ring of the blacksmith's anvil and were tempted to 'look in at the open door'.

The blacksmith was known to us all as Daddy Lloyd, a name he had acquired through being the only 'Daddy' in a district where all other fathers were either 'Dads' or 'Daddas'. Daddy was very fond of children, his face wearing a beaming smile whenever we were around.

The roar of his bellows reached our ears as we turned the penthouse corner, and we found him pumping away at the horn-tipped bellows-handle to fan the grey coals to glowing red. We watched him draw the white-hot iron from the fire amidst a shower of sparks and beat it to shape on the anvil. Around the walls of the forge hung horseshoes, hinges and other things he had made in his spare time, whilst a farm implement or two usually awaited his attention outside.

Daddy Lloyd.

Daddy Lloyd (right) holding horse's hoof.

Sometimes we arrived to find him with a horse's hoof in his leathered lap, filing it with long, steady strokes. We watched while the hot shoe was fitted, and smelt the acrid fumes which rose from the hoof. As the nails bit deep we flinched, expecting the horse to rear or kick, but Daddy assured us that horses' hoofs, like children's nails, had no feeling.

One day we arrived to find him banding a cart-wheel from the nearby wheelwright's yard. The wheel was clamped down on a circular plate, while a band, previously made to fit, was heating in the fire. Daddy pumped away at the bellows, from time to time moving the band to ensure it was evenly heated. When it was ready, several men grabbed it with tongs and rushed it out to the waiting wheel. There was a strong smell of burning wood as the hot band was hammered home. Buckets of water, standing in readiness, were thrown, hissing and steaming, over the wheel to contract the band and ensure a tight fit.

Just outside the smithy, hollow metal rails edged the road at the end of the bridge. Several minutes were always spent here 'telephoning' each other through the hollow rails. Telephones intrigued us, though I doubt if any of us had actually seen a telephone then. All urgent messages were carried by telegram from Kington five miles away. The arrival of the telegraph boy was greeted with alarm, for telegrams were never sent lightly and often brought news of death. The carrier waited while the message was read in case he was needed to take a reply.

When, a few years later, the telephone was installed at the post office, everyone was terrified of the thing and all gave their messages to the postmistress to 'phone for them. Everyone admired her courage in using it, though it was plain to see that she viewed her job with some apprehension. In time, one or two braver souls made calls themselves, having first been 'put through' by the postmistress. Most, having in mind the distance their message had to travel, shouted into the mouthpiece, deafening the receiver of the call and allowing their business to be overheard by folks outside the building. One man, discussing with his doctor his child's constipation problems, was evidently asked if the child had had his bowels opened. Much to the amusement of the eavesdroppers he was heard to reply, 'Well yes, doctor, 'e did dung a little morsel this morning.'

We never ventured into the wheelwright's yard, for Mr. Powell was always far too engrossed in his work to bother with children, but from the road we glimpsed his workshop and saw-pit and sometimes saw a five-barred gate, a wheel, a cart or even a coffin in the making.

In autumn, rosy apples lured us into the village orchards. Usually we were content to escape unseen with one or two, but one afternoon, in one of the village orchards where all the apples were high on the branches, stick after stick had to be thrown to knock them down. Suddenly a voice called, 'Come you on down through this gate.' Deeply ashamed, we hung our heads to hide our guilty, scarlet cheeks, and meekly left, wondering how we'd ever face old Mr. Thomas again.

Of course there was no shop on our direct route home, and none of us had ever heard of pocket-money, but in the village the small shop window drew us like a magnet. We pressed our noses against the panes with mouths watering for the goodies on display. One afternoon we turned from the window to see a silver sixpence lying in the road and could scarcely believe our eyes. In a trice we were in the shop and the sixpence exchanged for the mouth-watering delights we had hungered for but never hoped to enjoy. That day was counted a red-letter day, to be recalled time and again.

Reaching home meant changing into old clothes for work or play. This I loathed and longed always to wear pretty clothes like children in story-books. Each day in school I watched and romanticized over the Infant Teacher and envied what I considered to be her ideal life. When school was over she returned to her cosy digs to spend the evening as she pleased, with no one to insist that she changed into shabby clothes to do boring jobs. I envied her standing smartly dressed every day before her class, issuing instructions and going from pupil to pupil to see they were carried out. She had no worries like the rest of us, who came each day fearing we'd be called upon to do something beyond our capabilities. I was sure that all teachers hated having to give up the pleasures of teaching for weeks on end during the holidays. I longed to write exercises on a blackboard, to hear children read, to mark in red ink the mistakes in their books. I spent hours with my imaginary class imitating the teacher, and could think of no more interesting way of spending a whole lifetime.

13. Outings

Excitement tinged with apprehension wakened us early on this eventful morning of 25 June 1926, a morning of gilded mist that heralded a glorious day. For the first time we were to leave the confines of our neighbourhood and travel by motor charabanc to a faraway place called Llandrindod Wells. It was a notable day not only for children but for many adults also, who, until this day had travelled only in horse-drawn vehicles, and few to so distant a place.

Excitement robbed us of our appetites. The minutes passed slowly, the hands of the clock seeming reluctant to move. 'Isn't it time yet?' we kept asking. Finally the magic hour arrived when we put on our Sunday clothes and set off across Dol-garn pastures, still heavy with dew, cuckoos calling from every side.

Having wondered for days what a charabanc looked like we turned the Rectory corner to find it, with hood folded back, already waiting at the roadside. Many friends, all in their Sunday best, were already assembled beneath the giant oak that stood at the entrance to the village. The road was chequered with sunshine and shadow; wisps of dust whirled up on a cooling breeze that gently stirred the leaves overhead. Here amongst the grown-ups even the big boys looked small. All remained close to their parents, shy of greeting friends in the company of adults. Suddenly, from the door in the garden wall, the Rector emerged to marshall us on to the lawn, there to present us each with a shilling pocket money.

In the 'chara' the seat in the centre of each row was folded back to allow access to the rear and, as each row was filled, this was replaced and occupied, till the vehicle was filled to capacity. Then we were off, the good wishes of those left behind ringing in our ears.

In places the 'chara' brushed both banks of our narrow roads. Passing even a bicycle would have been impossible except in a few wider parts. Behind us clouds of dust rose from the unsurfaced roads. Our speed, necessarily slow in the narrow lanes, increased when we reached the main road at Walton. Never had we travelled so fast. Before reaching New Radnor a calamity of the first order occurred when a strong breeze carried off Mu's new hat. At that time anyone without a hat seemed only half dressed, so the loss cast a cloud over our day. There was nothing to do, Mother said, but buy a new one as soon as we reached Llandrindod.

From New Radnor the road climbed steadily to the Radnor Forest, where the narrow, hairpin bends were negotiated with interest and excitement. At Pen-y-bont puffs of smoke rose above buildings on our right and soon a train came into view. This, for children living so far from a station, was a rare sight, for some probably their first glimpse of a train. All watched the puffing engine with rapt attention as it ran parallel with the road practically all the way to Llandrindod Wells.

We found the Spa to be a grand place, with wide streets, huge hotels, boarding houses and neatly kept parks and gardens. There were so many things to see that we hardly knew which way to look first.

While the 'chara' conveyed the main party to the lake we alighted outside the Central Wales Emporium, there to buy the all-important hat. We recognised Mr. Thomas, who kept the Emporium, at once, for every year with the return of the swallows he paid us his annual visit. Putting up at the Royal Oak in the village, he trudged from farm to farm with his bundle on his back, inviting housewives to purchase his wares and help to lighten his load. On his arrival we waited expectantly for the pencil or other such welcome gift that he always brought. Afterwards we accompanied him a short distance on the way to his next port of call, helping to carry his pack. Was it because he was a vegetarian, we wondered, that he broke wind with almost every step, occasioning us considerable difficulty in suppressing the laughter that threatened to explode.

With a suitable hat selected and Mu once more respectable, we sallied forth to join the rest of the party. We found the lakeside alive with folk, some relaxing on seats, some strolling at the water's edge and some in motor-boats, chugging out over the sparkling water. Several of our party hired a boat, which rocked threateningly as we nervously embarked. Soon we too were gliding out over the cool, sunny water. Graceful swans, moorhens and ducks swam lazily across the lake. One brood of small ducklings followed their mother, equidistantly, in a straight line, looking like large, downy beads on an invisible thread. In the wooden shelters dotted along the shore, visitors to the Spa sheltered from the midday heat in the scent of the lime trees that fringed the banks. At the boat-house we paid our first visit to water-closets and were greatly intrigued.

After a picnic lunch on the lakeside common we saw, for the first time, tennis courts and bowling and putting greens. For the first time we walked along well-kept paths and over pretty bridges in a park resplendent with beds of flowers. At the pump-rooms visitors sipped mineral waters whilst enjoying the bracing air.

But all good things come to an end and the day, which in the morning had stretched endlessly ahead, came to a close. We said goodbye to all the fine sights and boarded the 'chara' for home. By now shadows stretched long across the fields and before reaching New Radnor all but the eastern slopes were grey in shadow. It was a quiet party, subdued by exhaustion and drained by excitement, that reached Newchurch in the brooding calm of the summer's evening, our thoughts full of the wonderful sights we had seen. It was difficult to say what had given us the most enjoyment, for all had been so strange and new and unlike anything we had seen before.

A surprise awaited us when we reached home, for there on the table was Mu's lost hat. Ours was a friendly, intimate world, where people's possessions were easily recognised. The hat had been recovered by a Kington lorry driver travelling in the opposite direction. Like everyone else for miles around he had heard of our outing to Llandrindod and he had returned the hat to Newchurch, where the owner had soon been identified. That day's outing gave us our first glimpse of life beyond our boundaries; our lives were never to be quite so insular again.

Two years later a trip to Aberystwyth afforded all children, and many adults, their first glimpse of the sea, which until the arrival of the motor coach had been beyond reach. Most of the older inhabitants died without ever setting eyes on the sea and perhaps had no clear concept of what it looked like. One old character we met on our way to the coach greeted us with, 'I warn you be off to see the big pool.' Perhaps that's how he visualized it.

That day's outing was not without its misadventures, for the coach fumes proved too much for many, including myself, as did our first boat trip. And during the day one grown-up member of the party found himself adrift from the main herd. The mischief had occurred when he paused to watch the Punch and Judy show and had turned to find nothing but strange faces. Frantically he searched in all directions, without success, till at last, in desperation, he approached a stranger, enquiring, ''Ave you sin anythin' of the Newchurch consarn?' The stranger was totally nonplussed and said he was afraid he was unable to help. 'Well,' promised the lost soul, 'if I can once get home to the Missus I'll see I'll never leave 'er again.' It was with great relief that he spotted a familiar figure in the distance and he lost no time in making contact with the rest of the party.

The homeward journey was broken to allow passengers their first visit to a fish-and-chip shop. One thirty-year-old passenger, on his first outing from home, eyed with suspicion the packet of chips handed to him by his mother. Noting his hesitation his mother yelled, 'Well, eat 'em, Thomas! 'Taters, 'em be!' Soon the packet was empty and Thomas smacking his lips in appreciation.

14. Summer Holidays

Until we were old enough to be of help on the farm, part of our summer holidays was spent with our Great Aunt and Uncle at a farm called Penwain, near Glasbury. On a Thursday, early in the holiday, we were taken by trap to meet Aunt Penwain in Hay. Nothing pleased us better than a trap ride through the scented summer lanes when dog-roses flowered the hedges and lacy cow-parsley decked banks brightened with foxgloves and ragwort. Sitting on the back seat we watched the white road run out, like a ribbon, from beneath the trap. Sheep, white from recent shearing, dotted the distant banks and the whirr of mowing machines filled the summer air.

Aunty and Uncle Penwain (they were never referred to as Aunty Margaret and Uncle Richard) awaited our arrival at the Black Swan, where Uncle's brother-in-law was proprietor. We soon espied Aunty's slight figure, dressed as usual all in black, her face covered by a black veil. She wore her clothes to almost ankle length, covering the tops of her high, kid, buttoned boots. Her kind, faded blue eyes smiled a welcome, and kissing her soft, wrinkled face was like kissing a crumpled rose petal.

People from all the neighbouring districts converged on Hay on market-day, ostensibly to sell their produce and purchase their weekly groceries, though the visit was actually as much a social trip as a business one, and as Aunty went from shop to shop she paused repeatedly to chat with friends.

Her first call was at the grocer's where, in an atmosphere permeated by a strong smell of coffee, mixed with a dozen other scents, a smiling proprietor chatted amicably with his customers, treating all with the utmost civility. Most of Aunty's requirements had to be weighed, some even blended, from the contents of various bags. The large raisins she bought had to be stoned before use. The candied peel came in large pieces with wells of melted sugar set hard in the centre. The grocer deftly made his own bags from blue sugar-paper, pouring in the weighed amounts before folding the ends securely. Provided Aunt gave the same order each week she knew to the farthing how much her bill would be, for prices never fluctuated. Before leaving, she bought us some toffee which the grocer, with his toffee-hammer, broke from a large slab into his scales.

At the butcher's fresh carcases, bought in the local market, hung from hooks to provide succulent joints from which none of the flavour had been

Auntie and Uncle Penwain.

lost by freezing or artificial feeding. There were dressed fowls—boilers and roasters; there was mutton as well as lamb. Outside, rabbits and game hung from hooks near the doorway.

We followed Aunty into the ironmonger's through a doorway festooned with clanging buckets, stable lanterns, scythes and bill-hooks. Inside were oil-lamps, shades and chimneys, candlesticks, knife-cleaners, cast-iron kettles, pots and pans. On their ends against the walls were zinc baths, fenders and fire-irons, and a host of other things no longer seen.

The really high spot of the day for us was the visit to the old café, with its sloping oak floors, where Aunty spared no expense on delicious white bread and butter and jam, fancy cakes and pastries that made our mouths water.

Though barely ten miles from Newchurch, the lush countryside around Glasbury, with its rich, red soil, contrasted sharply with the grey-soiled upland district where we had our home. Green and copper beeches, massive oaks and flowering chestnuts bedecked the parks and embosomed fine houses in immaculate grounds. Amongst all this lushness and fertility we felt we were in another world.

There was a long climb from the village to Penwain and we were glad to reach the pasture-gate and the footpath leading to the garden, with its pretty paths edged by low-cropped box-hedges and over-arched with rose bowers. At the sight of the young plum trees a guilty conscience brought blushes of shame to my cheeks: I remembered a previous visit when Aunty had caught me pinching plums and had tapped her kitchen window. I wondered if she remembered it too.

We were greeted at the door by a faint smell of beeswax. Annie, the maid, was laying tea and the kettle was singing merrily over the fire. As Aunty unpacked the shopping we followed Annie across the passage to the cool dairy to fetch a dish of sweet butter and a jug of ice-cold milk. In the shallow leads the cream had risen to the surface and was ready for Annie to skim. Back in the kitchen, Aunty brought chairs to the table from their places against the wall and we settled down to a second tea.

Uncle arrived, talkative and market-piert, having spent too much time in the Blue Boar. He scorned tea and made his way down the stone steps to the cellar for his customary jug of cider.

Tired after a long day we sat with Aunty in the deepening shadows beside the fire, the room full of glints and gleams of polished wood, brass and china, till it was time to climb the slippery treads of the old oak staircase and have a slide or two on the wide landing in our stockinged-feet on our way to bed.

To us the bedroom was quite luxurious with its carpets and large deep feather-bed, with snowy linen and white, honeycombed, deep-fringed bedspread. The large chest-of-drawers, with its dazzlingly white lace-edged cloth, displayed old family photographs in silver frames. The marble-topped washstand supported a flower-patterned ewer, basin and toilet set and beside it was a matching slop-pail. But what took our eye most of all were the large, globe-shaped glass ornaments on the dressing-table which, when inverted, produced showers of snow-flakes falling on the enclosed scenes. The windows commanded a splendid panoramic view of the wide Wye valley with its backcloth of mountains, a view that changed by the minute, as sunshine followed shadow.

We rose in the morning to find all windows thrown wide to welcome the sweet-scented morning air and Annie in rough apron scrubbing the already spotless flagstones, for in Aunty's house fresh air and cleanliness were the order of the day. The polished furniture shone to mirror-like brightness; the willow patterned dinner-service on the old Welsh dresser sparkled. Above the bobbled chenille mantle-drape the skillet and brass candlesticks flashed and winked in the firelight, as did the horse-brasses hanging down each side of the grate, the fire-irons and fender, the burnished oven-knob and boiler tap, and the jet-black range. A glistening grandfather clock ticked away the minutes beside the carved oak coffer, while the oak corner cupboard and china cabinet mirrored the leaping flames. A high-backed settle shielded the hearth from draughts and faced Aunty's cushioned wicker chair. Slanting sunbeams, streaming through the window, were hard pressed to find a dust-mote in their path.

After breakfast we followed Annie across the cobbled yard to the large, well-lit back-kitchen where all major jobs were done. A huge table, white and ridged with constant scrubbing, occupied the centre of the floor. In one corner, near the sink, was the furnace for boiling the clothes; nearby, the wooden mangle. Diagonally across the room was the baking-oven and alongside it the end-over-end butter-churn. In keeping with everything in the room, Annie's face shone as though polished. I wished we had a separate room like this at home, where all work could be done, so that the kitchen-cum-living room need not be disturbed.

Every Monday morning at Aunty's house all bed-linen was changed, though only creases distinguished the dirty from the clean. Nevertheless, Aunty invariably entreated Annie to be sure to sooble the clothes well, in several waters, before blueing them. Annie had been in Aunty's service since the age of twelve, however, and had long since grown as meticulous as her mistress, so the advice was patently superfluous.

Beside the garden wall a long flight of stone steps led up from the cobbles to the granary over the back-kitchen. Many a sunny hour we whiled away at the top of these steps, gazing at a breathtaking view that I found most comforting on our first, rather home-sick visit, for we had a distant view of the same mountains from the Banky Field at home. From this vantage point we often saw a tramp making for the kitchen door, where he knew he could be sure of the warm reception which many such had discovered in Aunty's warm-hearted generosity. Should he, however, have the misfortune to encounter Uncle *en route,* he would be summarily dismissed with, 'Off my premises!' Uncle had no time for 'idle louts living off other men's backs.'

Beyond the garden an orchard extended along the lane as far as Ciltwrch Common. Having no orchard at home, we counted it a great privilege to help ourselves to an apple whenever the fancy took us. Aunty discouraged any association with the children from the Common cottages, but when she was busy indoors we chatted with them over the hedge and furtively handed them an apple or two, feeling like queens distributing largesse.

On Sunday mornings we accompanied Aunty to her church, situated at the entrance of the drive leading to Maesllwch Castle. Once or twice, when taking a short cut to visit relations at Brynwrhydd Farm, we walked with Aunty the whole length of the drive, through well kept grounds and the Castle environs, to reach the Lodge gates at the further end. We found it a magnificent journey, quite unlike any walks we had previously undertaken.

Across the road from the church, in the grounds of a large house, several peacocks displayed their fine tails and rattled their quills. Several minutes were spent after Service gazing at these splendid birds.

In the evening there was a second long walk to accompany Annie to the Baptist chapel over the Wye bridge.

As the holiday drew to its close we were impatient to meet our parents, hoping that, while we were away, they had bought the baby we so badly wanted. At first sight of them, talking to a group of friends, we blurted out the question uppermost in our minds, 'Have you bought a baby yet?' For some reason everyone seemed to find the question amusing. Our hopes fell at the negative reply and all at once going home seemed less attractive.

As Aunty kissed us goodbye she cheered us up remarkably by giving us half-a-crown each. Aunty loved giving and in later years, when Uncle had retired and money was less plentiful, she was grieved when she could no longer reward each of our little services. Regretfully she would say, 'Many thanks, dear, but I don't know where you'll spend them.'

Every year, during our summer holiday, Aunty Emma and Uncle David came to stay at Penvain. We always looked forward to their visit, for both were very fond of children and made a great fuss of us. They never came without presents and before leaving always gave us several coins for our moneyboxes. Uncle David used to hold us in turn while we listened to the gold watch ticking in his fob pocket and played with the gold trinkets that dangled from the chain stretching across his chest. But before he released us he tickled us unmercifully, refusing to stop till we said, 'Stop your tickling, Jock!' Convulsed and weak with laughter, we found this extremely difficult.

Uncle David was a first-class painter and decorator and when the alterations to our house were completed he spent his whole holiday graining all the main doors. His excellent work can still be seen today.

* * * *

Summer would not have been summer without whimberry picking. Folks from almost every dwelling turned out in suitable weather to make a few extra pounds while they could. As soon as we were considered old enough to do our bit to augment the family income, much of our holiday time was also spent on the whimberry hills. We had several hills to choose from, Trewilliam, the farthest and most popular, being four miles distant.

Armed with a basket for the whimberries, cake-tins in which to pick them, macks in case of rain and a picnic lunch, we set out on hazy mornings over smooth elastic turf silvered with dew. We had but to touch the tall bents of grass or fronds of fern that edged the green ride to send showers of crystal dewdrops cascading to the ground. Our path followed the old stone wall along the edge of Newchurch Hill. On the right, green turfed banks and hollows gave way to gorse and bracken stretching away to the top of the hill. Here and there on the dewy turf dark patches marked the spots where sheep and mountain ponies had lain to rest the previous night. Everywhere white scuts flashed as grey-brown rabbits hopped in the hazy sunshine. In the distance the Black Mountains and Brecon Beacons were wrapped in a soft blue haze.

Near Green Lane Cottage we met a neighbour riding his old carthorse to the smithy. 'I warn you be off whimberry scrattin'?' was his greeting. We told him he was lucky to be riding while we had to walk. 'Aye,' he replied, 'but this ahld 'orse is too wide in the back, yer can hardly stroddle 'im. Yer might as well try to ride a 'ill.'

As we skirted Bryngwyn Hill we could see many pickers on its steep face.

Occasionally a grouse rose from the ride and flew away low over the heather. On the crest of the hill we could see the shooting-butts, already in position for the twelfth of August, when beaters would drive the grouse into the cruel gunfire of the local squires and their guests.

We took the shady lane down to the Upper Glasnant, where we stopped for a chat with the Jones family. We loved the two little girls, Rita and Dot. Three-year-old Rita was a cuddly, round-faced mite with big brown eyes under a brown fringe. Dot, somewhat younger, was a dainty child with golden ringlets. We always longed to take one of these cherubs home with us and were thrilled one day when tiny Rita said she would like to come. We were very afraid that once out of sight of home she would panic and want to return but she chatted away quite happily without any qualms. She stayed with us overnight and would have stayed even longer if, fearing her parents might be anxious about her, we had not delivered her back the following day.

From the Upper Glasnant we followed the brook up a picturesque valley where alders spread their shade. Tall bents and high bracken, laden with dew, overhung our grassy path, saturating our plimsolls and drenching our dresses to the waist. Some distance up the valley we crossed the peaty brook on insecure, squelching islands of rushes and climbed steep fields through thickly growing, downy thistles on which flocks of goldfinches were feasting. Overhead, buzzards climbed, with scarcely a flap of their powerful wings, to soar majestically, uttering their mournful 'see-i-oo, see-i-oo'. By the hill gate feathery larches swept over the fence. The air was full of murmuring flies, droning bees and chirring grasshoppers. We found a pleasant spot beneath a stunted hawthorn beside a stream to deposit our impedimenta. Here, in the shade, we would have our lunch when the sun had reached its zenith and heat shimmered on distant banks. Our faces lit up as we espied our friends Gladys and Gwen coming down a path through the heather. All day we four worked side by side, picking the blue-black berries and chatting the time away. The hillside was dotted with pickers, most of whom we knew and with whom we had a chat before the day was through. Whilst enjoying our meal in the shade we discussed past events and local people. A neighbour who had a large cyst on his head was brought into the conversation. We wondered how the barber managed to cut his hair. 'Oh,' said Gladys, 'I warn the barber cuts a back-swath round the lump first, like the men do round the meadow.'

On our homeward journeys we sometimes came upon swarms of ants dancing in the evening air. This was the month of their nuptials. Some, their honeymoon over, had dropped to the ground to form dark patches on the green ride; others, still dancing overhead, landed on our heads and shoulders. Frantically we brushed them off and left the path to avoid them. A couple of days later we pondered over the scores of tiny transparent wings that littered the path, ignorant of the fact that, courtship over, the female ants had bitten off their wings for life underground.

Tired and hungry we were glad to reach the bank above the well and hear Mother's cheery greeting from the open window. The drawts was brought out to weigh our whimberries and our efforts were duly applauded. We sat down with ravenous appetites, to home-cured ham and new-laid eggs, new potatoes and garden peas, followed by apple tart and custard. No meal ever tasted better. Our whimberries joined those of other pickers on the market stalls in Hay. Though the dealers paid but a few pence a pound, we earned several pounds during the season, a small percentage of which reached our money-boxes.

15. A Big Surprise

One golden October day in 1923 Mu and I were surprised to find ourselves taken to a ploughing match. The field was a hive of activity, with men, horses and ploughs and knots of people dotted around the headlands. Each team shone with careful grooming, their plaited tails and manes bedecked with coloured braids, their polished harness ablaze with burnished brasses. Apart from these splendid creatures there was little to interest two small girls. We idly watched as each team strove to plough a winning furrow and listened with scant attention to the comments of those around us. As the minutes dragged by we browsed in the hedges for nuts and blackberries.

After what seemed like hours we espied Dad coming in at the gate and rushed to meet him, quite unprepared for the sensational news he brought. He told us that the doctor had been to our house and had brought a baby in his black bag. We were utterly astounded and overjoyed and could scarcely be restrained from running the whole way home.

When we burst into the kitchen our high spirits were momentarily checked on coming face to face with a strange lady who smilingly enquired if we wanted to see our new brother, telling us we would find him upstairs in Mother's bedroom. Upstairs we flew, stumbling in our haste, and tumbling into the bedroom found the new baby in Mamma's arms. I was quite taken aback and, though I would never have admitted it, somewhat disappointed, for instead of the chubby baby with sparkling eyes, golden curls and pearly teeth that I had expected, I saw a red-faced mite with toothless gums and tight-shut eyes, crying and squirming in a large white shawl. A fire burned in the bedroom grate. Mamma turned back the baby's long nightie to show us his tiny toes and wee toe-nails. His soft, boneless-looking legs protruded from a large white nappy. His tiny body was wrapped round and round with a binder. Mamma allowed us to hold him in turn. I was amazed to find him warm, soft and quite heavy, so unlike our dolls. He writhed in his shawl, threshing his arms and legs about. I quickly handed him back, fearing he'd wriggle out of my arms. Beside the bed was his cot, with pillow and cot-clothes.

We were surprised to learn that Mamma and the baby were to be upstairs for some time, while we were to be looked after by Granny and the strange lady we had met in the back-kitchen.

Eventually the day arrived when Mamma and baby were expected downstairs, and a wooden cradle with a wooden hood was placed near the hearth to receive our new brother who, by now, was looking a little more like the baby I had visualised. For a while he was a great novelty. We spent all our time gazing at his tiny hands and fingernails and stroking his silky blond hair. Gradually the novelty wore off and drawbacks began to emerge. This new brother, we found, captured all the attention. So much time and care was lavished on him that we began to feel neglected. Every time Dad came in he went straight to the cradle to bill and coo. Every visitor fussed over him. We were jealous that his merest whimper brought Mamma running to caress and soothe him. We were often called to rock the cradle, and I soon got tired of that game! If he was not asleep in a very few minutes I grew impatient and rocked violently, hurling him from side to side. Far from sleeping, he cried all the more, bringing Mamma to comfort him and scold me for my impatience. Before long our play was interrupted by calls of, 'Come and mind the baby.' All in all, instead of being the kind of live doll which I had imagined, he was proving an encumbrance. There were dirty nappies and wet bibs—all quite unforeseen. Only when he started taking notice of things and trying to talk did he become more interesting.

One day, when he had reached crawling stage, Mamma put me in charge of him in the far passage where there was nothing for meddlesome fingers to play with and where she was sure we could come to no harm. I lifted him up onto the wide window-sill where he could see the animals in the farmyard and sat beside him as he cooed happily, beating the panes with his chubby hands. Suddenly he knocked the latch and before I knew what had happened had disappeared through the open window. There was quite a big drop to the yard outside and several cart-horses galloped past as he fell. For a moment I stood petrified, then ran to tell Mamma. I found her talking to Granny in the kitchen and, having been taught never to interrupt a conversation, I waited, sick with worry till Mother turned to find me behind her. Almost before I had blurted out my alarming news she was out of the kitchen, followed by Granny, leaving me waiting for I knew not what, too stunned even to dwell on the punishment that would surely be mine. What enormous relief flooded through me when Mamma returned with the baby, apparently little the worse for his fall. Everyone found it incredible that he could have fallen from such a height onto a hard surface without apparent injury. Even though the horses had galloped over him, they too had left him untouched. Either because of her overwhelming relief at the outcome, or because she held me blameless,

Mamma never even reprimanded me. The dreadful incident taught me a hard lesson, however, and from that day I took my responsibilities very seriously.

Until we were allowed to take him outdoors to see the birds and animals and watch the outdoor activities, we entertained Billy with nursery rhymes and alphabetic picture-books. When he felt under the weather, though, he wanted only Mamma, who would cradle him in her arms and sing the old ditty:

Little Billy's sick, sick, sick.
Send for the doctor quick, quick, quick.
The doctor came with a rap-a-tap-tap,
Walked in the room with his stick and hat,
And told little Billy's Mamma
To keep him warm and still;
And when I come tomorrow,
You must pay my great big bill.

How proudly we showed him to our friends on the first Sunday he was allowed to accompany us to Sunday School. Each friend, in turn, shook him by the hand, enquiring, 'How are you today, Billy?' To each he patiently replied, 'Belly mell tank oo.'

When he was ten years old, I stood one afternoon by the kitchen window watching the branches of the sycamore at the foot of the fold bending and tossing in a ferocious gale. Indignant hens with ruffled feathers were driven, protesting loudly, before the blast. Billy was battling his way to the barn when a fierce gust tore from the roof a large tile which struck him on the head, throwing him to the ground. My scream brought everyone to their feet. They rushed to where Billy lay, senseless, in the mud and gently carried him indoors, blood streaming from his head. The doctor diagnosed severe concussion and advised complete rest and careful nursing. When the wound had healed a pronounced dent was left in his skull. This, the doctor feared might, as he grew, press on the brain. He was therefore admitted to hospital to undergo the delicate operation of having this dent straightened. He bears the scars to this day.

16. 'Shades of the Prison House'

By degrees the carefree days of early childhood ebbed away to be replaced by more jobs and responsibility. With the perversity of human nature all the jobs we had so clamoured to do in our playhouse now seemed irksome and boring. Indoor jobs were especially tiresome. Bedmaking we loathed, especially in winter when the bedrooms were cold and the bedclothes icy. Instead of getting the job done and off our minds, we sat on the bedside, bemoaning our lot, till Mother called to know what we were up to. Outdoor jobs, like feeding the hens and collecting the eggs, were much more to our taste, for there was usually something of interest to see.

Before we had proper fowl-houses we had to make a daily round of barns, sheds, haylofts and other places where hens had established nests, occasionally coming unexpectedly upon a new nest brimming full of eggs. This caused enormous excitement and we felt praise was due as much to us as to the hens.

Occasionally a hen became broody and 'stole her nest' (i.e. laid eggs away from her usual place), giving her secret away by clucking as she joined the rest at feeding time. It was our job then to keep an eye on her movements, hoping to be led to the nest. But all such hens were very wily and would peck nonchalantly around till they found our guard momentarily relaxed and, in a trice, disappear. When the nest was finally located, the eggs were removed and the hen shut in the uncomfortable sloping hay-rack of a sheep cratch till she had lost her broodiness and was content to lay in the established nests.

We fed the hens with oats scooped from the golden pile on the granary floor, or with maize which was kept in a deep zinc bin away from rats and mice. When the corn was low in the bin I was obliged to jump up and balance on the bin-edge in order to reach it. More than once I came perilously near to landing head-first in the corn.

As we approached with the food, cackling hens came running and flying from all directions; one or two bolder ones even flew up to land on the bucket rim. The corn having been scattered, contented clucks came from all sides as busy beaks pecked away. The meal over, they wandered off with long, drawn-out squawks of satiety and lament which seemed to say, 'Ah, that feels better, but we would have appreciated a bit more!'

Each week, as baking day approached, we were called upon to tush gorse stems to heat the oven and pick up chips left by the men when hedging.

We also collected dead sticks, known locally as chats, for kindling. We saved Mother many a step by reaching and fetching and running errands to the village and neighbouring farms. Year by year the errands were extended to more distant places hitherto unvisited by us. Before we set out Dad gave us careful directions as to the shortest route, via stiles and foot-paths. Roads were rarely made use of. Not a single signpost existed at that time throughout the neighbourhood, for local folks needed no directions and strangers were never seen. These distant errands broadened our horizons, gave us a sense of adventure and exploration and provided novel glimpses of nature's wonderland.

Bringing the cows home to be milked afforded a pleasant, leisurely stroll on a fragrant summer evening. I loitered down the lane beside the stream, lost in thought, with just Meg, the dog, for company. Most of the cows were already at the gate, lowing loudly in answer to their calves in the pens. Those with no calves were in no hurry and still grazed leisurely at the far side of the field. The sight of Meg speeding towards them soon brought them galloping towards the gate, puffing and grunting with the unaccustomed exercise, their swollen elders swinging from side to side.

Having to crowd together in the narrow lane gave the bossy ones the opportunity to hile the more timid ones, forcing me to bring my stick down hard on the offenders' backs to maintain law and order. Daisy and Violet, two matronly Hereford cows, looked disdainfully down on the younger showoffs. They were past such skittish behaviour. Poor Daisy had a dislocated hip and walked with a limp. She had learned early that life could be a grim affair. One by one they entered the beast-house, each to wait in her accustomed place to be secured with a heavy tie-chain.

During the winter months sheep had to be driven from field to field to find fresh pasture. Hay, cake and oats were taken to the sheep cratches and trows to keep them in good condition for lambing. Compared with today, farms carried relatively small flocks. We knew all our sheep and could have recognized any one of them in a strange flock; their faces, to us, were just as recognisable as people's.

It was also our job to feed the tiddling lambs with bottles of cow's milk. Perpetually hungry, they almost knocked us over in their eagerness to get the teats in their mouths. They sucked ravenously, wiggling their tails the whole time. When the bottles were empty they nuzzled up our skirts, looking for more. These lambs became sportive and playful and loved to boont people with their heads. It was great fun seeing an unsuspecting person charged from the rear, especially if he was caught bending, but somewhat less amusing to find oneself on the receiving end. I would go far out of my way to avoid a grown tiddling but they held no fear for Mu, who would jump on their backs, hold on by their ears, and ride them round and round the fold.

In winter, when men were busy foddering the animals, Mu and I were called upon to pulp turnips or mangels for the cattle. It was in jobs such as these that we so missed an elder brother. We loathed this dirty, cold job and envied the village children, snug in their cosy cottages with no such unpleasant tasks to perform.

Often on cold grey afternoons we had first to collect the turnips from the cootch in the rickyard, spearing them with dungforks to fill the wheelbarrow, which we took turns in wheeling down the steep slope to the barn. In bitter weather the exercise gradually warmed us till our numbed hands and feet tingled and burned.

When tea was over we sallied forth, lantern in hand, across the fold flooded with soft light from the kitchen window, for blinds were never drawn at night. The light from a lantern suspended from a beam in the barn penetrated the darkness of the adjoining byre, picking out the white faces of the cows in the booseys, their limpid eyes staring expectantly. A rich smell of hay emanated from the overhead loft to mingle with the smells of barn and byre.

With dungfork in hand, one set about feeding the pulper while the other turned the handle. Our huge shadows, climbing the walls, bent and stretched with every movement. Tempers flared when a turnip became wedged in the pulper in such a position that the blades failed to chop it and the whole pulperful of cold, muddy turnips had to be removed to reach the offender. Our every movement was followed by the cows who, dribbling with anticipation, turned their heads from side to side and rattled their tie-chains. As we approached with a succulent bucketful they blew heavily through their nostrils and their warm breath caressed our faces.

While the cows were slavering over their succulent meal, we pulped for the bullocks in the shed across the fold. These were large animals, almost ready for market; we could sense their massive weight as they brushed against us. Several bucketsful were spread along the manger and sprinkled with meal before the wide gate was flung open and the eager animals, blowing and snorting, allowed to rush in. One never-to-be-forgotten evening I was still at the manger when Mu, thinking I was close behind her, opened the gate. In rushed the snorting bullocks, side by side in a line. I quailed at the sight, expecting to be crushed to death against the stone wall but, providentially, they crowded to the far side, allowing just enough room for me to squeeze past. What a fright it gave us! It was a mistake never repeated.

The farm animals held little fear for Mu but, having at an early age been punished by a gander's steel-hard wings and by a tiddling's iron-hard head, I remained nervous. Returning one evening from the fowl-house, I turned to see a cart-horse racing after me with bared teeth and ears flat against its head. I ran for my life with little hope of outpacing my pursuer, and, crossing a muddy patch, slipped, throwing up my hands to keep my balance. This sudden movement stopped the horse in its tracks. But for the muddy patch, perhaps those angry teeth would have gripped my shoulder and thrown me down to be trampled to death. This same horse startled us on another occasion when the cart-horses were driven into the fold. Possibly a dog nipped this particular one, making it dash for the nearest opening, which chanced to be the gate leading to the open kitchen door. Before we realised what was happening the huge creature was standing beside the kitchen table like the proverbial bull in the china shop. We stood rooted to the spot, afraid almost to breathe lest it should rear or kick and smash everything to smithereens. Luckily Ernie, the waggoner, was at hand to soothe the beast and slowly coax it through the door before any damage was done.

In spring a blitz was made on the oonts or moles which sent up oonti-tumps all over the fields. Sometimes the oont-catcher was employed to set traps in the mouths of the mole-runs, but a simpler and less expensive method was to put down poisoned worms. To our dismay the job of collecting the worms was delegated to Mu and me. On a raw, grey morning, clad in old coats, we reluctantly made our way along the road by the rickyard hedge, hunching our shoulders against the cold, to reach the hoar-frosted field beyond.

The ploughman was already at work, occasionally directing his team with 'See, Bonny' or 'Come here, Duke' as he strove to plough a straight furrow, struggling at the same time to keep his footing in the trench he was creating. It was our job to follow the plough and collect the worms turned out by the ploughshare. With freezing hands and feet we trudged along the furrow, each clutching a tin in a cold stiff hand. Behind us screeching gulls dived and swooped, to settle on the furrow and snatch the worms we had missed. How we detested the feel of those wriggling creatures! We snatched them up quickly and dropped them into the tins, only to find them crawling out again and having repeatedly to be thrust back. What a luxury it was to run home when the task was completed, wash our aching hands in warm water and toast our frozen feet on the fender before a blazing fire.

Our village shop was open all hours, with the occasional customer arriving as late as ten o'clock at night. One of my more pleasant jobs was the weekly trip to fetch the yeast for baking. In winter I skipped the whole way, arriving all aglow and tingling with warmth. The homeward, uphill journey took much longer, for there were snail shells, faded by exposure to light and weather, to be searched for. There were holes in the banks to be pondered over, wondering what small creature had its home inside. There were ice-covered potholes to be stamped on to break the glass-like ice, and smooth patches of snow to be imprinted with footmarks. I loved yeast and stole from the packet as much as I dared. In February or March I found the first green leaves of the dog's-mercury, though I did not then know its name. I welcomed it as the first messenger of spring. Later the lacquered celandine shone in the sun, soon to be followed by the primrose and violet. In summer, when the banks were ablaze with wild flowers, I collected a colourful bunch for old Mrs Thomas who lived at the shop. Sometimes I was allowed in to present my bouquet personally and would find her in a back room, seated beside the fire in her wicker chair and wearing a cream-coloured mob-cap edged with lace. Her dark full-skirted dress with its cream modesty vest reached the floor; her puffy hands rested on the arms of her chair. On the wall behind hung a picture which I took to be her photograph. Years later I was to discover it to be an ageing Queen Victoria. The likeness was quite remarkable. Sometimes I was rewarded with a packet of sweets from the shop. Though this was greatly welcomed, it robbed me of the virtuous feeling I had enjoyed in doing a kind deed unbidden. In all my journeys I rarely met a soul on the road.

One spring afternoon, when returning with the yeast, I espied a chaffinch's nest in the hedge and eagerly scrambled up the slippery, rain-soaked bank to take a peek inside. Both my feet slipped and I fell heavily, striking my left eye on a hedging stake. Oh dear! what had I done? I slipped down, holding my injured eye, wishing there was someone at hand to tell me what it looked like. It was too painful to close and my first thought was, 'How shall I manage to sleep?' I hurried home to Mother, confident, as always, that she would know what to do. She gently lifted the upper lid to reveal something dark beneath. As it was too painful for further investigation she was considering sending for the doctor, when a loud barking of dogs and a tap on the door announced the arrival of Daddy Lloyd, the village blacksmith. Daddy was well known for his natural remedies, and seeing my white, anxious face, enquired what was wrong. When he heard my story he gently took hold of the upper eyelashes and, pulling the lid away from the ball of the eye, inserted his tongue and gently and painlessly licked out several splinters. What relief to be able to close my eye in comfort again! With regular bathing and the protection of an eye-shield, the blood-red eye gradually returned to normal. Everyone said I had been extremely fortunate; many had lost an eye in much less dangerous accidents.

Mu used to collect Granny's pension and carry it in a small bag with draw-strings. One day, on her way home, she whirled the bag round and round her wrist on the strings. Faster and faster she whirled it until, without warning, it abruptly left her wrist and took wing to a high branch of a sycamore tree in the hedge. Poor Mu stared and stared at the bag, willing it to fall. She threw stone after stone to dislodge it, but all to no avail. There was nothing for it but to go home, own up and face the music. When the row was over a man was sent, with a long pole, to retrieve it. Mu was in disgrace.

17. Sundays

The Sundays of our early childhood were very special, quite unlike the ordinary days of the week. Sundays were sacred and solemn Sabbaths—to be hallowed; games were forbidden; only vital jobs were done. No one would have dreamed of sewing or knitting; any garment needing repair was attended to by Saturday night or left till the following week. Sunday was the Lord's Day, set apart for prayer, worship and rest.

Preparation for this all-important day commenced on Saturday, when Sunday clothes were overhauled and Sunday shoes polished. The weekend joint was cooked, to be eaten cold for Sunday lunch. On Saturday night the large galvanised tub was placed before the kitchen fire for the weekly baths. All must be clean for Sunday.

Over the years, however, strict Sunday observance was gradually relaxed till it became customary, for instance, to see the waggoner's bicycle up-ended on a sack on a Sunday morning, its inner tube hanging out, ready for the puncture to be repaired. Another occasional Sunday morning job was hair-cutting, for in the country each man was the other's barber.

When animals had been tended, men shaved the week's stubble from their faces with leather-stropped cut-throat razors. Later they exchanged their weekly shirts with a stud in the neckband for Sunday shirts with detachable collar and tie. When they had donned their blue serge Sunday suits they were barely recognisable as the men who, a few hours earlier, had sat down to breakfast in weekday garb. This day of rest had been looked forward to all the week. Their ditty ran:

Saturday night is my delight
And so is Sunday morning.
Sunday night comes far too soon
And beggar to Monday morning.

In the early days, whatever the weather, the family, except for Granny (who was C. of E.), drove the four miles to Painscastle Baptist Chapel for afternoon service, stabling the pony at Pendre Farm in the village and occasionally staying to tea with the Lloyd family after service. In cold weather the waterproof, blanket-lined trap rug kept us cosily warm on the journey. This same rug and a large trap umbrella kept us dry when it rained. On fine days the journey was one of pure pleasure.

After a few years arrangements were made for the Painscastle Baptist Minister to conduct morning service in Newchurch School. The congregation occupied the school desks, the teacher's desk serving as the pulpit. As there was, initially, no piano, Dad led the singing with the aid of a tuning fork.

We sadly missed our weekly trap ride, setting out on foot together over the hill along our usual school-day route. On our return we were invariably confronted with a cold hearth and the task of rekindling the fire and coaxing it with the bellows, before the vegetable pot was ground down on the coals to boil quickly and satisfy our ravenous appetites.

When lunch was over, Mu and I set off for Sunday school in the small Presbyterian chapel in the village. It never occurred to us to stay at home, for we had never known Sunday afternoon to be spent in any other way. Light-heartedly we skipped off by the top pool, disturbing ducks sleeping on the water or standing on one leg on the banks, all with heads tucked beneath their wings, their reflections mirrored in the sunny surface. Down by the garden-side we bent our steps to the lower pool, where, on sunny days, the elm tree's shade dappled the white geese on the water. At the Poolpiece gate we took the footpath through Dol-garn pasture, chatting busily as we went. The journey took longer in summer, for then there were stitchwort seedboxes to pop, dandelion clocks to blow, foxglove flowers to burst between thumb and finger, and ear-splitting noises to make by blowing blades of grass between thumbs.

As we reached the bend of the last hill the slate-blue spire of the little church came into view, rising up behind the old yew tree, by the churchyard gate. At the foot of the hill the Rectory, sheltered by several trees, stood back behind its lawns on the left corner of the T-junction, facing the apple orchard across the road. Through the apple trees an ancient farmhouse, Great House, could be glimpsed overlooking the churchyard where, for almost five centuries, it had watched generations come and go. We welcomed every opportunity of visiting the village, for though but a hamlet of some half a dozen houses, to us it was the hub of the universe. Outside the Rectory garden wall, at the centre of three converging roads, stood a giant oak. Years of use had worn down the surrounding roads to leave it standing, amidst exposed roots, on a mound. This was the rendezvous where young men lounged to chat on summer evenings.

Our chapel was small, but there were even smaller 'tin tabernacles' buried in the hills, where literate Sunday school teachers were hard to come by. In one such chapel 'twas said that when the children, reading in turn from the Bible, came upon a difficult word, the teacher, ignorant as the pupils, advised them to 'miss 'im an' go on to the next'. What sense could be made of a lesson with so many omissions can only be guessed at; the poor man did his best.

At our chapel gate we met our friends and climbed the shallow steps to cross the lawn together. Inside, the small, box-shaped building was cream-washed from the brown match-boarding to the white ceiling. The seats, arranged at right angles to the door, faced the small pulpit, in front of which was the American organ, its back to the congregation. One large window on either side of the door, and one in the opposite wall, provided ample daylight. At night the room was illumined by two large paraffin lamps suspended from the ceiling, augmented by two globed lamps, one on either side of the pulpit. In the centre of the room a small Tortoise stove stood on a stone hearth let into the floor.

According to the season we either chatted around the stove or sat in the seats until our instructors, Mr Powell, the wheelwright and Mr Lloyd, the blacksmith, arrived to teach us the scriptures. Bible readings were discussed and questions put to us, but uppermost in our minds, especially in summer when sunshine streamed in through the open door, were thoughts of how we would spend our time when school was over.

After school we loitered awhile on the pretty stone bridge by the smithy, gazing over the parapet at our reflections and spotting trout in the crystal-clear water. After a while we had the illusion of sailing away upstream on the bridge as the current flowed beneath it. We threw in small sticks, running to the opposite side to see whose stick appeared first.

Occasionally we ventured into the churchyard and wandered waist-deep through the feathery grass amongst tombstones of different heights and sizes, leaning at various angles, but all facing the rising sun. We read the epitaphs, once in a while coming upon a name we knew. Here we paused to speculate on the body under the green mound before pensively moving on. Near the gate the giant yew leaned over the path but we knew nothing of 'fair Emmeline' who slept in the grave beside it. Several years were to elapse before she was immortalised by the publication of Kilvert's Diary just before the Second World War.

One Sunday we came upon the parson's surplice lying in the road. One of the party donned the vestment and prepared to address the rest but before he could commence the sermon the parson rounded the corner in search of the missing article. All hung their heads in embarrassment, while the wearer shamefacedly handed it over, more than likely to the secret amusement of the owner.

On returning home we went straight to our bedroom to take off our

Mr. Powell, wheelright and Sunday School teacher.

Sunday clothes. In the intense silence of the late afternoon I always fancied I could hear distant music and persuaded myself it was the angels in heaven playing on their golden harps.

It was considered unlucky not to wear something new on Easter Sunday, perhaps because Easter was a time for joy and celebration. Christ had risen and death had been conquered. All nature reawakened to join in the praise. Regular attenders at Sunday school were presented with prizes. It was an important day for children like us whose presents were few and far between. Proudly we carried our trophies home and on the fly-leaf beneath our names wrote:

Steal not this book for fear of shame,
For here you see the owner's name:
And when you die the Lord will say,
'Where is that book you stole away?'
And if you say you cannot tell
The Lord will cast you down in hell.

or, in a less-prized book:

If this book be found to roam,
Box its ears and send it home.

The outstanding day of our Sunday school year was the Sunday School Anniversary. For weeks prior to this event we practised our recitations and songs with Miss Bryan, the organist. Besides being tested in Sunday school, Mu and I had 'to go through the mill' a couple of times a week at home. 'Now,' commanded Dad, 'stand up, put your shoulders back and speak out.' When our enunciation and expression were as good as he could hope to get them we were told that it would have to do. But we were left in no doubt that it was, regrettably, very far from perfect. Preference was usually given to uplifting or improving poems and those with a moral. Some of the older folk favoured tear-jerking poems of affliction or bereavement, like 'Little Jim', the story of the death of a miner's only child, which, with tear-filled eyes, the listeners pronounced 'Very cutting.' I can still recall most of the poems I recited; the following is an example:

Wishes of High and Low.

A man in his carriage was riding along,
A gaily dressed wife by his side;
In satins and laces, she looked like a queen,
And he like a king in his pride.

A wood-sawyer stood in the street as they passed;
The carriage and couple he eyed,
And said, as he worked with a saw on a log,
'I wish I was rich and could ride.'

The man in the carriage remarked to his wife,
'One thing I would do if I could,
I'd give all my wealth for the strength and the health
Of that man that saweth the wood.'

A pretty young maid with a bundle of work,
Whose face, as the morning, was fair,
Went tripping along, with a smile of delight,
Whilst humming a love-breathing air.

She looked on the carriage, the lady she saw,
Arrayed in apparel so fine,
And said, in a whisper, 'I wish for my heart
Those satins and laces were mine.'

The lady looked out on the maid with the work,
So fair, in her calico dress,
And said, 'I'd relinquish possession and wealth,
Her beauty and youth to possess.'

Thus, in this world, whatever our lot,
Our minds and our times we employ
With longing and sighing for what we have not,
Ungrateful for what we enjoy.

We welcome the pleasures for which we have sighed,
But the heart has a void in it still,
Growing deeper and wider the longer we live,
Which nothing but heaven can fill.

For weeks we looked forward to the Anniversary, always visualising it in sunshine, for then it was held out of doors, attended by a large congregation. The chapel seats were arranged facing each other across the path, on the green in front of the chapel; the organ stood on the path before the door.

All day our excitement knew no bounds, till, when the time came to start for the village, it was almost unbearable. With pounding hearts we set off, proud as peacocks in our new outfits, wondering what our friends would be wearing, hoping their dresses would not out-do ours. The first people to arrive occupied the 'grandstand' seats up on the lawn; the rest assembled on the low bank across the road. There was no traffic at that time and as everyone from far and near would already be present, no interruptions could be expected to disturb the service.

The opening hymn, from 'Sankey and Moody', was sung with great gusto and enjoyment. Then, with butterflies in our tummies, we sat on the front benches, waiting for our names to be called. Face after face was recognised in the large congregation, for though many had travelled considerable distances few were strangers to us. For the choir items we had each other's support but facing the congregation alone, to say our recitations, was quite an ordeal for shy country children. The worse part, so far as I was concerned, was knowing that the moment my name was called colour would flood my cheeks. I would have given anything to be able to stand before a crowd without blushing. Only when my turn was over could I enjoy the others' recitations and the solos, duets, trios and quartets that went to make up the programme.

Group at Newchurch. Girls in front row, from left to right:
Gwen, Kathleen, Mu (with Billy), author, Gladys.

Group in quarry, Newchurch. Girls standing in front, from left to right: author, Kathleen, Gwen, Mu, Gladys.

Too soon the doxology and benediction brought the Anniversary to a close. Now we looked forward to the tea and sports the following day. Trestle-tables were set up in the chapel and people fed in relays, children first. We made short work of the boughten cakes, thinly cut white bread and butter and sandwiches which most of us tasted only on occasions such as this. I well remember my first piece of chocolate swiss-roll; to me, used only to home-made yeast cake, it was sheer ambrosia—a taste never to be forgotten. We left the table 'full as ticks', to link arms with our friends and wander up and down the village in blissful happiness, making sure we saw everyone and that we were seen by all.

When all had been fed, the whole assembly flocked over the bridge by the smithy and turned in at a gate that led through trees to the old quarry near the village well. Here, in a picturesque setting, we stood on ledges of rock, tier behind tier, for the annual photograph. The photographer set up his tripod and after some changing of plates and several dives under the black cloth, all was ready, and one click gave us a pictorial record of the day.

By the stepping stones everyone then crossed the stream that trickled down through the alders from the village well to the river and made for the field where the sports were to be held. All children were lined up according to age for the various races. The first home received threepence, the second two pence and the third one penny. Next came the teenage races, followed by the Mothers' and Fathers' race and the race for the over-sixties. Spectators sat on the grassy bank beneath the wood, shading their eyes against the lowering sun. Plagued by gnats, they persuaded pipe-smokers to join them to disperse the insects with their smoke. Games such as Nuts and May, Oranges and Lemons and Twos and Threes followed the races. Then came the all-important football match, which, though not exactly a first division performance, was nevertheless enjoyed by spectators and players alike. Finally, all children were rounded up and presented with a packet of sweets before reluctantly leaving for home.

For the young men and maidens the best was yet to come: no local sports ended without Kiss-in-the-Ring. Eyes sparkled with excitement and anticipation as the ring was formed. When a man was nominated to circle the ring to select his maid, all the girls furtively watched his progress, wondering if she would be chosen. The selected girl, having received his kiss, then circled the ring to make her choice by tapping a man on the back and running off. He, giving chase and catching her, tried to plant his kiss on her lips as she buried her face in her hands. What fun and merry-making abounded! The attractive lassies had more than their fair share of kisses, while their plainer pals had to be content with few. The nearby woods echoed to the laughter, as droll, side-splitting comments and instructions came from the wits in the ring. Twilight gathered and the moon rose to light up the ripples in the river, casting soft shadows across the silvered grass and clothing the nearby woods with ethereal beauty. How conducive to romance was such an enchanted setting! Fun continued till night dews drenched the grass, when couple after couple left the ring and crossed the moon-dappled stream beneath the alders to wander in close embrace through the chequered copse, thence to make their homeward ways through moonlit lanes and fields.

* * * *

By the time we had reached our teens, small country churches were rapidly losing their hold over the community. Many that had once employed both vicar and curate were now unable even to support a vicar and the benefices of neighbouring parishes were linked. The joint incumbency of Bryngwyn and Newchurch was given to the Bryngwyn vicar and Newchurch Rectory was put on the market.

Dad, who by now was spreading his wings somewhat, having purchased a small adjoining farm, decided to buy the Rectory too, and Aunty and Uncle Penwain, who were retiring from farming, came there to live. These arrangements delighted Mu and me, giving us something we had always longed for—a footing in the village—a pitch in the very heart of things! Not only this, but it provided an excuse for an occasional visit and the chance of lingering awhile, *en route,* with some current heart-throb.

We were now allowed, albeit rather reluctantly, to attend Sunday evening service in the little chapel in the village. This simple outing gave us immense pleasure and was looked upon as the regular highspot of the week. As Sunday evening approached we had difficulty suppressing our excitement at the thought of a few hours free of parental restraint, in the company of friends. Our parents, suspicious of our high spirits, wondered what we got up to when out of their sight. The quiet countryside, in their opinion, provided ample opportunity for young folk to 'overstep the traces' and they wanted no disgrace brought upon the family. Before setting out we were sternly warned to conduct ourselves decently and to be home in good time. We knew better than to disobey.

On Sundays, as in the week, it was our duty to shut the fowl-houses for the night. This took a considerable time, as the houses were situated in fields some distance apart. On shorter days it presented no problem, as we allowed ourselves time to do the job, but in summer the hens were in no hurry to go to roost and tried our patience exceedingly. One or more were sure to be still pecking around when we arrived, and should they so much as catch a glimpse of our approach their excited cackles brought all the others off the roosts, delaying us even further. So we approached with caution and waited, out of sight, in feverish impatience, till the last one had disappeared through the pop-hole, then crept up and slammed down the door. Hurrah! Free at last! But not before we had run the gauntlet of the crowd of men who lounged every Sunday evening under the village oak, to comment on all who passed, could we really feel free and relaxed to enjoy the evening.

By going to chapel we made several new girl-friends who, though they lived locally, had attended different day-schools. We also made the acquaintance of boys who gathered in the village on Sunday evenings. This was the only regular opportunity the sexes had for meeting.

Sitting amongst friends, all full of youthful exuberance, waiting in silence for the service to commence, the slightest thing tickled us. On fine evenings the boys remained outside, their laughter occasionally reaching our ears, but on cold, wet winter evenings several sought shelter inside, bursting through the door in a kind of bashful bravado, to make for the back seats. One at least was sure to have squeaky boots which sparked off our giggles.

One local preacher put us under great strain. His beaming, jovial face was amusing in itself. As he rushed excitedly from one end of the pulpit to the other we held our breath, expecting him to take one too many steps backwards and tumble down the steps. Whilst waving his arms about one evening he knocked the Bible shut and lost his text. Later he really excelled himself by gesturing expansively down over the front of the pulpit and knocking the organist's hat askew. This taxed the composure of even the most staid in the congregation.

Perhaps to capture the attention of the younger element, he introduced his text one evening in rather an unusual way. He told the tale of John and Mary, who had been 'keeping company' for some time. Mary was confident in her own mind of John's love but was concerned that after several years there was no sign of a proposal. Searching her mind for something to do about this, she at last hit upon a plan. 'John,' she said as they walked together, 'I am thinking of getting married.' John was thunderstruck. 'Oh, Mary,' he replied, 'this *has* come as a shock. Who is this man you intend to marry?' Handing him a slip of paper, Mary said, 'When you get home, John, turn to this passage in your Bible and you will find the answer.' On reaching home John rushed for his Bible and turning up the relevant passage, sighed with relief to read, 'Thou art the man.' Those words became the text for the evening.

On moonless winter nights we emerged from the service into utter darkness, each conscious of unseen eyes upon her as she was framed for a moment in the light of the doorway. There was keen competition for the privilege of escorting us home and until we had fixed on a particular escort we were followed by a dozen or more. On dark nights when someone came forward from the group to try his luck by walking alongside or taking an arm, it was difficult to distinguish his features and maybe he could be identified only by his voice. We found these dark, faceless followers somewhat intimidating but knew that we could rely on the local lads to see we came to no harm.

On summer evenings, when young men travelled long distances to size up the local girls, I, and no doubt others, hoped to find some strange Adonis in the crowd who would flutter my heart and fall for my charms. Outside, the girls grouped together to chat awhile, conscious of the men's intent gaze. Occasionally stolen glances were exchanged between the sexes before the girls parted company, to go their separate ways, followed as always by a band of men.

Occasionally, during the summer months, we travelled further afield to anniversaries in neighbouring parishes, thereby widening our circle of friends and acquaintances. Those summer outings, in the palmy days of adolescence, were sheer bliss. Keyed up with expectations of pleasures to come, we set out over soft, springy hill paths or along leafy lanes to some distant chapel. There, amidst rows of friends enjoying the anniversary programmes, our thoughts kept straying to the fun still to come when, the anniversary over, we set off home—a group of starry-eyed lasses followed by a throng of jolly lads. Feminine chatter was punctuated by masculine quips and jokes. Our radiant faces testified to the joy these simple pleasures brought. The longer the journey the better we were pleased. To be happier would have been impossible: our joy was complete.

At each road junction a certain gaiety departed with those whose path lay in another direction. All too soon the numbers dwindled. If the chapel visited lay on our side of the village we had a few girl friends all the way, but if beyond the village the last of the friends departed some half mile before the journey's end, taking with them the remaining joy and cheer. Without their support we felt bashful and embarrassed by the attention of the following men.

One particular evening, when followed by an unusually large crowd, our courage failed and on reaching the village we took refuge in the Rectory. When, after an hour, the place was still surrounded, we persuaded dear old Aunty, small and frail though she was, to accompany us the rest of the way. Her presence, we felt sure, would scatter the escorts. Not a bit of it; undeterred they still followed the whole way before accepting that the game was up. On returning through Dol-garn pastures they helped themselves to a fowl from the hen-house and carrying it squawking to the village, hurled it through the door of a cottage, frightening the sole occupant out of her wits. Of course the news of the incident spread and we had to live down taunts of having to bribe boys with a hen in order to persuade them to escort us home. This is the only occasion I can recall when any kind of mischief was done.

* * * *

An important event in the annals of the Baptist Church was the baptismal service, when candidates were initiated into church membership. Small country chapels boasted no indoor baptistries, so immersion

A baptism in River Edw.

took place in the river. People came for miles and lined the river banks to witness the ceremony. It was customary for females to wear white dresses with small lead weights in the hems to prevent them from rising in the water; men wore ordinary suits.

The minister waded out into deep water and, one by one, candidates were escorted to him by a deacon. After quoting appropriate words of scripture, the minister plunged each candidate backwards, totally immersing him, while the assembled congregation sang a suitable chorus. As each candidate reached the bank, a cloak was thrown over his shoulders and he was accompanied to an appointed house to change in readiness for the following service, when he would be received into church membership.

Baptismal services were sometimes held in the spring when the water was still extremely cold, indeed even fringed with ice as it was when Mother was baptised. Though candidates baptised in such conditions often had to walk considerable distances in wet clothes before they were able to change, I have never heard of anyone suffering ill effects as a result.

Mu was baptised in the River Arrow below Newchurch School, quite close to the spot where several years earlier I had fallen in during the dinner hour. The shock of the icy water made her gasp for breath as she reached the deeper part. My turn came a couple of years later at Gladestry, on a fine sunny day. I well remember wearing a pale green slip under my white dress for the occasion and being embarrassed to find the colour showing through the white dress as I came up out of the water.

18. Away to School

In 1929 Newchurch School held its first entrance examination for the County Secondary (Grammar) School. Several pupils sat but only two passed—not surprising in view of the low standard of teaching we had received for most of our time at the school. The two successful pupils, of whom I was one, were offered places at Llandrindod Wells County Secondary School. My place only was accepted.

My last day in the Primary School was a sad one. It was difficult to believe that I would never sit in that classroom again or accompany my friends down to the river at dinnertime. Would there really be no more journeys along the velvet path through the scented bracken? The thought of saying goodbye to all that had been my life for so long made me sick at heart and I had difficulty in choking back my tears. The hymn chosen for that day was:

Jesus, friend of little children,
Be a friend to me;
Take my hand and ever keep me
Close to Thee.

Teach me how to grow in goodness,
Daily as I grow;
Thou has been a child and surely
Thou dost know.

Step by step, oh! lead me onward,
Upward into youth;
Wiser, stronger, still becoming
In Thy truth.

Never leave me, nor forsake me,
Ever be my friend;
For I need Thee, from life's dawning
To its end.

This hymn, I felt, had been chosen especially for me, launching out into the unknown. I made it a prayer from my heart.

All through the summer holidays, as I helped with the jobs on the farm, I idly wondered what the future held and what life would be like in the County School. I knew no one who had attended a secondary school; to me it was a closed book. I felt I was the local pioneer, braving the unknown that others might benefit from my experience. I vaguely pictured the new school as a one-roomed building like Newchurch School—perhaps a bit larger and having a few more pupils. I looked forward to the adventure in an apprehensive kind of way but had no real fears. But relinquishing the security of home and a neighbourhood where every person was a well-known friend for a life amongst complete strangers was a trauma I had not anticipated. Only when my parents had left me in my digs did I realise how utterly alone I was and how very much I missed them.

There were in the digs six other girls from outlying districts, three newcomers like myself and three older girls. On that first evening we laid out our school uniforms ready for the morrow, but my blazer; which should have been delivered by post, had not arrived. 'What are you going to do?' enquired the older girls. 'They are very strict about uniform, you know.' I worried all night, imagining myself standing out like a sore thumb amongst all the blazered girls, wondering what my punishment would be. Great was my relief, the following morning, when the postman arrived with the all-important parcel just as we were about to set out for school.

The other new girls in the digs had older sisters or acquaintances from their own localities, so I felt very much the outsider. When we reached the school grounds scores of pupils were laughing and chattering outside the Girls' Entrance. Older girls introduced their young sisters or friends. I knew no one and waited apart, self-conscious, friendless and dejected. The security of home seemed worlds away and I yearned for the sight of a familiar face. Feeling small and insignificant, I wondered what these seemingly self-confident girls, whom I took to be from the posh houses of Llandrindod, would think of my humble background and the lowly folk I called my friends.

There was a mad rush when the doors were opened. The new pupils, myself excepted, were shown around by their sisters or friends. Pegs were found for them; toilets and classrooms pointed out. I tagged on behind, doing the best I could by listening to what others were told, getting more bewildered by the minute. Thoroughly confused by so many rooms, I found myself being herded, with other newcomers, into the assembly hall for morning prayers.

After the service all newcomers were taken upstairs to the science laboratory, there to give their names and other relevant information to a mistress who was obviously bored to tears at having to confront a motley crowd of greenhorns at the end of a pleasant holiday. She rapped out questions and to every answer made a sarcastic retort. I felt lost and terrified. Eventually half the assembly was assigned to Form IIa, while the rest, including myself, were escorted to Form IIr by the irate female who was to become our form-mistress. Under her snappish instructions we were required to make something called a time-table to pin inside our desk-lids. It was the first time I had heard of a time-table and I had not the vaguest idea what was required but was, of course, far too frightened to ask. None was completed to her satisfaction, for she terrified us out of our wits.

It was a huge relief, at the end of that first harrowing day, even to return to strange digs; but how daunting to realise there would be countless similar days to follow. We were relieved to learn from the older girls that the fiery female who had made our first day such a nightmare would not be teaching us regularly, but only for art and P.E. When I found the other new girls to be as scared and bewildered as myself I felt we had something in common and sharing the day's experiences brought us closer together.

Grammar School friends (author at front of row).

When tea was over the older girls took us to see the lake and the town but I took little pleasure in the sights, for gnawing homesickness accompanied every step.

Our lodgings was a semi-detached boarding house called Loretto, which comprised a lounge and dining-room on the ground floor, four bedrooms and a bathroom on the first floor, and attic bedrooms above. Our meals were served in the basement kitchen, where a green-tiled cooking range kept the room pleasantly warm. From the adjoining scullery a door led to the paved back-yard, with its shed and toilet, and to the vegetable garden beyond. Our main meals were supplied by our landlady, Mrs Powell, but we were expected to provide our own suppers. Each week, through the post, we each received a cooked chicken or joint of meat which was kept down in the ice-cold underground pantry reached by several steps from the basement kitchen. The pantry floor was alive with cockroaches which crunched beneath our feet. Only ravenous hunger drove us down, for how we detested the sight and feel of those insects!

The bedroom which I shared with three other girls overlooked back-yards, gardens and steep fields climbing up towards the lake. It was furnished with two double beds, a large communal chest-of-drawers topped by a swing mirror held in position by a wad of paper, and a wash-stand with ewer and basin. A curtained recess was our only wardrobe. We washed in cold water from the ewer, each pouring the used water into the slop-pail beside the wash-stand. 'Bags first washing in the morning!' cried the first one to remember to do so as we undressed at night. 'Second!' 'Third!' chipped in the others. No one liked washing last and having to hurry down to breakfast.

Together we set out for school in our pleated navy gymslips (one inch above the knee), white blouses, blue and yellow striped ties, black, woollen gym-stockings, navy blazers and caps adorned with the school badge, and black laced shoes. Navy gaberdine raincoats protected us in cold or wet weather. Woe betide anyone caught minus a single item of this uniform, either in school or walking in the streets. For physical training, gymslips had to be three inches from the ground when kneeling. This rule, like all other, was stringently enforced.

Play-times, however cold, were spent out of doors; only during heavy rain were we allowed to remain in our classrooms. Discipline was strict, talking in classrooms and corridors forbidden. Running in the corridors was also forbidden and anyone breaking the rules was detained after school. Persistent offenders were dispatched to the headmaster's study for the cane.

Newcomers from small country schools found most teachers signally stern and strict, and were it not for the kind face and reassuring smile of Miss Evans, the cookery mistress (who is still alive as I write, having reached her 103rd year), life in those first bewildering weeks would have been unbearably cold and hostile.

Pupils were required to provide their own textbooks and equipment. Only exercise books were provided free. Because everything had to be paid for from slender resources, we valued our possessions and treated them with respect. When possible we bought second-hand books from the previous year's students and sold our own to those in the form below.

The school had no playing-field of its own in my early days there, but rented one wherever it could. At one time our hockey pitch must have been little short of a mile from the school, compelling us to run through the streets and the Rock Park to ensure enough time for a game when we reached it. Worse still was the uphill run back to arrive in time for the next lesson. Everyone tried to snatch a quick drink at the chalybeate spring in the park as we passed. Tennis was played on the town courts if we were lucky enough to find one empty.

Each day at lunch-time, and again when school was over, the covered entry that linked our digs to the house next door echoed to our footsteps as we raced for the back yard. After tea in the basement kitchen we settled down around the large table in the dining-room to do our homework.

On fine evenings when we had little to do, we strolled down into town to gaze in the shop windows, sometimes calling at the small shop near our digs for a penny apple or a halfpenny stick of liquorice. Very occasionally, when finances permitted, we occupied a cheap seat in the cinema, at first to see silent films and later 'talkies'. Films transported us into a wonderful world of excitement and opulence, holding us spellbound. We were deeply moved by the rapture or pathos portrayed and furtively wiped away the falling tears. As the film reached its climax we sat tensely on the edge of our seats, fearing for the safety of the hero or heroine. We need not have worried, for the most dire perils were always overcome and right invariably triumphed over wrong. We idolised the stars, identifying ourselves with the heroines, striving to emulate them in looks and character and model our lives on theirs. In fact, they had no small influence over us, and being invariably upright and chaste were an influence mainly for good.

On cold or wet evenings when homework was done, Mrs Powell joined us in a game of cards around the fire. When she was busy in the kitchen we buried our heads in romantic novels, though these were discouraged. One evening we were lost in our stories when Miss Evans, the senior mistress, was announced. We hurriedly sat on our books and tried to look angelic. Unfortunately, every chair in the room was occupied and someone had to rise to offer the visitor a seat. The forbidden literature was exposed and stern advice given to read more worthwhile books and spend more time on homework.

On summer evenings we loitered around the lake or played games on the lakeside common. The Spa, then in its heyday, was crowded with visitors taking the waters and enjoying the bracing air. Every hotel and boarding house, including our own, was full. We had to vacate our bedrooms for the guests and repair to the attics where, instead of going straight to bed, we got up to all kinds of pranks. We had great fun watching the drunks emerging from the Ridgeboure Hotel across the way, staggering and plaiting their legs up or down the street. From our dormer window we dropped small balls of paper on the heads of unsuspecting passers-by, amused at their bewilderment as they vainly tried to discover from where the missiles came. As soon as we heard Mrs Powell's step on the uncarpeted attic stairs we dived, fully clothed, into bed, pulling the bedclothes well up to our chins and struggling hard to suppress the laughter that bubbled up within, while she scolded us for making too much noise and disturbing her guests. Poor woman, how heedless we were of her cares and problems.

A tall, raw-boned woman, Mrs Powell had a pronounced stoop. Vestiges of a former beauty still lingered in her thin, high-cheekboned face. Her thin, grizzled hair was dragged back into a small bun at the back of her head. Even when she smiled, her faded blue eyes were grave, there being little in her hard life to bring a sparkle to them. Like many a widow of those days she had a hard struggle to make ends meet. Throughout the holiday season, besides preparing our meals till the term ended, she cooked three meals a day for her six or seven guests and served them with afternoon tea. There were many steps to climb from the basement kitchen to the dining room with heavy trays; more again to the bedrooms on both floors with water for the ewers, before descending, after bedmaking and dusting, with the slop-pails. The guests' every whim had to be pandered to, to ensure their return and recommendations. Empty rooms meant ruin. Every evening she looked dead-beat and must have willed her guests to retire early that she might fling herself down for a few hours on her own make-shift bed and take the weight off painful feet covered with corns and calluses and disfigured by large bunions. What relief it must have been to see the end of a successful season with a few extra pounds in her pocket and find at last a chance to relax after so many gruelling weeks.

A kind, conscientious landlady, Mrs Powell looked after us well. Anxious that out parents should feel they were getting value for money, she heaped our plates with Sunday lunch, insisting that every scrap be eaten. When the meal was over our stomachs were so distended that we almost saw stars, being then advised to 'run it off' up and down the entry before starting for Sunday school.

Once, when Sunday school was over, the Rev. Bee invited us into the Manse for tea. The window of the room where the tea was laid was at pavement level and we could see only the legs of passers-by. I always maintained that I could recognise any acquaintance by their legs, and when I observed the French mistress's legs passing I dealt my neighbour a kick under the table, nodding towards the window to draw her attention to this. Soon another pair of well known legs passed by and once again I delivered blows on her ankles. Only after leaving did I discover that I had not made contact with either of the girls but had, apparently, been raining kicks on the legs of the Rev. Bee. He said nothing: what he thought he kept to himself.

When the busy summer season was over, Mrs Powell at last found time to think of her painful feet. She had no money to spare for chiropody, even if such practice then existed, so I was invited to cut her corns and toe-nails and dress her painful broken bunions. Why this dubious honour was conferred on me, when there were older girls in the digs, I cannot say; perhaps she thought me the least likely to refuse. Her big-toe nails were so hard and horny that they were almost impossible to cut; moreover they both seemed to be loose and had to be held firmly while cutting. What suffering she must have endured throughout the summer months, spending hour after hour on those feet.

Poor Mrs Powell was constantly haunted by thoughts of a future when ill-health or age would prevent her from earning a living. There were no social security benefits to fall back on then, and no homes for the elderly. 'Never mind,' she was wont to say, 'I know Mona will look after me when I'm too old to work.' We took this as a joke but, looking back, I sometimes wonder if she secretly nurtured some vague hope that I *would* care for her in old age. I am ashamed to say that, callow and thoughtless, with many interests and excitements in life, I seldom thought of Mrs Powell when school-days were over and I don't know what ultimately became of her.

During my first year in the County School, I, and all the girls in my digs, returned home only for half-term breaks and end of term holidays. There being no public transport in the heart of the country, Dad was obliged to meet me with the trap several miles from home. Often I travelled on the bus over Radnor Forest to be picked up at a place called Walton, but occasionally I accompanied a friend, Olwen, to Hundred House near Builth Wells and was collected from there.

One homeward journey from Hundred House I shall never forget. Dusk was already falling as we made our way along the narrow lanes to the village of Glascwm. Beyond the village the steep, unfenced road ran along the hillside. On our right, heather-covered slopes climbed steeply to the skyline; on our left the narrow road was edged by a cliff. Half way up the hill Dad lost his glove and in the half-light we groped around the trap-bed to find it. On sitting up we were alarmed to find the off-side wheel on the very edge of the cliff. I froze in terror but Dad kept a cool head and gently reined the pony back. Another second would surely have plunged us, perhaps to our deaths, into the gorge below. With enormous relief we resumed our journey, thoughts of what might have happened sending shiver after shiver down my spine.

How joyfully I welcomed the summer holidays at the end of my first school year. What bliss it was to relax in the restful atmosphere of home. I had found the first term exceedingly exacting, setting out for school each morning tense and apprehensive. Much that had been revision to other pupils had been new to me, and my inherent lack of confidence did little to help. In my second term, when all pupils started more or less on the same footing, I fared better, viewing each coming day with less misgiving. When, at the end of the final term, examination results pronounced me top of the form, I was absolutely amazed and deep down felt sure someone, somewhere, had blundered. Perhaps someone had: I was never again able to test myself against the same pupils, as I was transferred to an 'A' form, where I had to compete with keener brains, and never quite reached that exalted position again. I looked forward eagerly to imparting the good news to my parents when I reached home but when I alighted from the bus at Walton, more than six miles from home, a woman greeted me with, ''Ello, I 'ear you be top of the tree.' The news had overtaken me and was already common knowledge, despite the fact that both public transport and telephones were still non-existent in country districts.

19. Fresh Arrangements

One day during the first summer holiday, Dad, returning with meal and flour from Rhos-goch Mill, brought the news that Anne, the miller's daughter, who had attended Painscastle school, had passed the entrance examination for the County School at Llandrindod and that arrangements had been made for the two of us to travel home at weekends. Had such an arrangement been possible during my first homesick year I should have been delighted but by this time I had made firm friends with the other girls in the digs and our weekends together had been great fun, so this news was not too well received.

On the first morning of the new term I was collected by taxi at 7 a.m. and was joined by Anne at Rhos-goch. We boarded the train at Erwood, transferred to a bus at Builth Wells and reached Llandrindod in time for 9 o'clock school. At the weekend we left after tea on the service bus for Builth, where, after an hour's wait, we boarded the train for Erwood, there to be met by Jack and his taxi which took us to Rhos-goch. From there I walked the two miles home.

On cold winter mornings, waiting for the taxi at the lane gate was a chilly experience. With no heater in the car we grew colder with every mile, and by the time we reached Erwood station were chilled to the bone. Needless to say the warmth of the railway carriage, as it carried us up the pretty Wye Valley to Builth, was greatly appreciated. In icy conditions Jack was afraid to risk the steep, winding, fenceless road down Sunnybank to Erwood and dropped us off at the top. We made good use of this opportunity to loiter down the hill and arrive at the station just as the train was leaving, ensuring for ourselves a morning's freedom.

One bitterly cold morning Mother and I waited at the lane gate with no sign of the taxi arriving. We were about to give up and return to the house, when we heard the car in the distance. Jack arrived in a flurry, having overslept. We raced off along the narrow winding roads. Anne joined us at Rhos-goch and, for the sake of warmth, squeezed in beside me on the front seat. Just beyond Painscastle we sped down the steep slope and on the blind corner at the foot met a motorcycle. Jack, swerving to avoid it, came to an abrupt halt in the ditch, shattering the windscreen and almost catapulting Ann and me through it, gashing her face and my knees. Nothing daunted, we extracted ourselves from the ditch and raced for Erwood, only to find the train gone. Jack gave chase to Builth. Shivering with cold, Ann and I held our blazers to the shattered screen in a vain attempt to keep out the freezing wind, while our battered vehicle, with its headlights facing the sky, attracted the attention of one and all. At Builth, finding the bus gone, Jack again gave chase and overtook it on the Llandrindod road. Passengers stared aghast at our battered car and dishevelled appearance, eager to know the cause.

As the weeks went by our travelling arrangements turned out to be somewhat unpredictable. Jack proved to be extremely forgetful and was rarely at the station when the train pulled in. As there were no 'phones in the country at that time we could contact neither him nor our parents. All we could do was to set out on foot, hoping to meet him round every corner. Once or twice we were completely forgotten and had to walk the whole way. I did not arrive home until 10.30 p.m. No one worried unduly when we failed to show up at the usual time, for the roads were traffic-free and the only folk we'd be likely to encounter were local people. Except for the occasional tramp, strangers were never seen.

In summertime I loitered awhile with Ann at her home, the picturesque old Rhos-goch mill, wandering by the mill-pond and watching the overshot wheel emptying its buckets in a rainbowed spray. Perhaps we'd pop into the mill itself and find old Mr Powell, with his long beard, bending over his work. Everything in the mill was dusted with meal and flour, which scented the whole place. Here, in ancient times, 'twas said, fairies danced on the mill floor to the sweet music of fiddles while the old miller slept in the mill-trough. Mr Powell, Ann's grandfather, paused in his work to chat awhile as he had done in bygone days when, as 'a handsome young man with a fine open face', he had paused in a romp with a child to talk to Francis Kilvert, the Diarist, on his first visit to the mill in 1870.

Just beyond the village of Rhos-goch the red, boggy moor which gave the place its name stretched for a mile or more on one side of the road. Clouds of black-headed gulls rose into the air, swooping and screaming over their nests on tussocks of rushes. Occasionally a skein of mallards would be outlined against the sky.

In winter, the countryside was black when I got out of the car at Rhos-goch to walk the two miles home, but gradually my eyes became accustomed to the darkness and I could make out the curve of the road ahead. But one night it was so pitch-black that I could see nothing and kept stumbling into the hedgebank every few yards. There was nothing to be done but persevere, hoping that Mu would soon turn up with the lantern to guide me. I had no fear of the dark. Half-light was more alarming than complete darkness, for then 'imagining some fear, how easy is a bush supposed a bear'. I had no fear of oncoming footsteps but wondered whom they would bring and, more importantly, what I would find to talk about when we came face to face. I always felt inadequate when conversing alone with adults, fearing that what I said might sound silly to them. I have never quite lost that fear. Sometimes the person could be recognised only by his voice, it being too dark even to see his outline.

One particular Friday evening Jack, who was a part-time bus driver, forgot us again until, driving through Builth with a load of passengers for the Police Ball in Llandrindod, he espied us ambling up the street, killing time till our train was due. What was he to do? He had to deliver his passengers. To our great delight he decided we'd have to accompany them. Gleefully we boarded the coach and returned in high spirits to Llandrindod, where Jack obtained permission for us to sit on the balcony in the Grand Pavilion to watch the dancers. It was our first visit to a ball, and how we enjoyed it! We watched enthralled as men in immaculate evening dress and white gloves guided gorgeously clad ladies through the maze of dancers. Jack brought us refreshments and from time to time came for a chat. We could hardly believe our luck! When the ball ended at 2 a.m. we were not in the least tired. The journey home was novel and exciting till our eyes became heavy with sleep. I knocked my surprised parents up around 4 a.m. As I had not arrived at my usual time they concluded that I was spending the weekend with one of my friends, as I sometimes did. What a story we had to tell our friends the following week!

When I reached my mid-teens Mu made a habit of walking towards Rhos-goch to meet me on Friday nights. It was not long before this became known and a couple of admirers took the same route. After several days spent apart, we sisters had lots of news to exchange and found these men a bit of a nuisance. One moonlit night, when a light fall of snow covered the ground, we decided to make a detour through fields to avoid them. Unfortunately, the snow masked a patch of boggy ground that lay in our path and before we could stop ourselves we were ankle deep in squelchy mud which sucked off one of my shoes. My next step landed my stockinged foot in the icy mud. In the dim light we had quite a problem in locating the missing shoe, which we eventually found full of water. Needless to say I had a less than comfortable journey home.

At this time, of course, we were still spending four nights in digs. By now we had made friends with girls from other digs, whom we met in the evenings and got up to all kinds of pranks. It was all harmless fun, with no destruction or vandalism of any kind. One night, for instance, several kept guard while one of the number switched the public library lights off at the mains, plunging all readers into darkness, while we escaped into the concealment of the grounds. Groping his way to the door, the old librarian yelled, 'All right, I know who you are, you'll be reported, and don't you dare to darken these doors again!' We knew that he would not have recognised us in daylight, much less in the dark, but even so entered school rather apprehensively the following day, fearing our escapade had by some means reached the headmaster's ears.

I recall strolling one summer evening with my friend Dot along the path bordering the lakeside common, when we came upon a dozen or so bicycles lying against the bank, obviously belonging to the footballers. 'Let's let the air out of the tyres,' suggested Dot. We set to work with a will and as we straightened our backs from the last wheel saw several men heading towards us. Not daring even to look round, we raced for the ladies' toilets in the park, there to wait with bated breath till we judged the coast was clear.

Talking or fraternising with boys was strictly forbidden. Even so, on winter evenings we recklessly ignored the consequences and met our sweethearts in shelters near the lake, where, for a few short, ecstatic moments we held hands and whispered sweet nothings, on tenterhooks the whole time lest someone in authority should spot us. Had such misdeeds reached the headmaster's ears we would have been threatened with expulsion or our parents informed, which would have been equally disastrous.

We so enjoyed our evening escapades that we rushed through our homework, helping each other with the difficult problems in order to get out quickly. Consequently the standard of work suffered, and I (and no doubt others) slipped down several positions in class. I well remember taking home my school report at the end of one term, knowing it would not please Dad, especially the bit at the foot of the report that said: 'Number of times detained for misconduct or neglect of work during term — 2'.

Ann too was concerned about her report, and in the end anxiety and curiosity overcame prudence. We sat on the bank, while waiting for the taxi, and opened the envelopes, creating, as we did so, the new problem of having to explain why they had been tampered with. We found no cheer in reading the remarks on the reports.

In school, by this time, those looking for mischief had discovered, in one of the older teachers, a weak disciplinarian and set about making his life hell. So many queer things found their way under his cushion that he hardly dared sit down. Pictures of scantily clad females adorned the desk when his lesson was due. One day a large jar of flowers, well-filled with water, was placed on the window-sill above his chair; a length of stout cotton, tied under the rim, was directed inconspicuously to a distant child. No sooner was he comfortably settled than a slight tug brought the jar down, drenching him to the skin. Feigning concern, one boy rushed to close the window, blaming the breeze for the catastrophe, while another sped to the rescue with a duster to mop his saturated suit. Another day, pausing on his way in, he accused someone of striking matches. All wide-eyed and innocent, we assured him he was completely mistaken. Fuming with rage he brought his hand down sharply on the desk, yelling, 'I thought I heard a noise, now I distinctly hear a smell!' The roar following that remark almost raised the roof. Poor man, how he must have welcomed retirement.

As time went on and more and more children passed the entrance exam, school buses were provided, enabling all pupils to travel to and from school daily. Our bus started from Kington and travelled via Newchurch, Painscastle and Clyro and thence up the Wye valley to Builth Wells, carrying pupils for both Builth Wells and Llandrindod Wells County Schools. The daily journey took us through some of the most beautiful scenery in the British Isles.

I was the first passenger, boarding the bus at 6.50 a.m. In winter, as I dressed by candlelight, the shiny black window panes mirrored everything in the room. Mother rose soon after 5.30 a.m. to light the fire and prepare breakfast. One morning, when not her usual bright self, she poured my tea, by mistake, into the sugar-basin, exclaiming, 'Well! Look at that!' before dissolving into laughter. After breakfast we set off down the lane

School Bus passengers (author, in centre, with clasped hands).

together, with the bright moon's reflection mirrored cold in the icy waters of the lower pool. The sky was ablaze with stars and our footsteps rang on the frozen lane. There was abroad the stillness of a world not yet awake. Not a creature stirred save a few ghostly sheep moving silently across the meadow's brow. Our voices sounded loud in the stillness as we waited, for what seemed an age, with no sign of the bus. Deciding we had missed it, we returned thoroughly chilled and fed-up to the warm kitchen, there to find the clock saying 6.00 a.m. We had been waiting, in the cold, an hour too soon—small wonder we had had the world to ourselves and that Mother had not been her usual bright self at breakfast time.

Occasionally, when the bus-driver returned to our vicinity in the small hours with a load of passengers from a ball, instead of returning to the depot in Kington for what little was left of the night, he would park his bus at our lane gates and take a couple of hours' snooze in Dad's chair, the door being left unlocked for him. In the morning he tapped the ceiling with the broom handle to waken me, while Mother prepared breakfast, after which we set off together for the bus at the lane gate. In bitter weather I persuaded Ann, when she boarded at Rhos-goch, to sit on my ice-cold feet.

Some mornings a hoar frost glistened on tree and hedge, transforming an otherwise dead landscape into a sparkling fairyland. On the homeward journey trees etched the delicate tracery of their branches against a pale evening sky, to lend to the scene a suggestion of peace and tranquillity. At other times of the year we reached the brow of the Begwns, above Clyro, to see day break over the Wye valley or to witness the sun rise over Cusop Hill, shedding colour and warmth in its path.

Wild, wet, windy days tossed and swayed the branches of trees, while rain lashed the misted windows on which we wrote messages to each other or rubbed clear patches to see hedges hung with raindrops and cattle and horses hunched with their backs to the rain-laden winds. The rain-pitted River Wye was swollen and brown with soil washed down by its tributaries. Turbid water foamed white over boulders and overflowed into sheets and pools where the banks were low. Low branches, half submerged, bent with the force of the current.

Spirits rose when April's sun slowly unfurled the leaves and wakened the countryside from its long winter's sleep. Small timid creatures, emerging from hibernation, were once more seen about their early morning business before the rush of the day began. In clear, transparent air, sunshine chased shadows across the mountainsides. Sometimes, near Erwood, the heron, still as a statue, stood knee deep in the river shallows, his keen eye alert for unsuspecting prey. If disturbed by our approach, he would lurch off with a 'kronk kronk' to try his luck elsewhere.

Though winter was reluctant to release its grip on the upland districts, May brought soft colour to the valley with apple blossom, flowering-cherry, lilac and laburnum. Near the end of the month the almond scent of may was overpowering. Each day more and more leaves opened, providing a myriad shades of green; horse-chestnuts lit pink and white candles to add yet more colour. Sometimes an angler could be seen here and there along the river banks, casting his line over the water. Near the ferry where a child crossed the river each morning to board the bus, we once watched the landing of a large salmon on the roadside verge, flapping and leaping at the end of the line. June days flamed with roses; bracken slopes put on their freshest green. Balmy air, laden with fragrance, caressed our faces through the open windows.

The homeward journey to Builth Wells was flanked by upland pastures, stunted oak-woods and distant mountains. Beyond Builth we followed the sylvan Wye for several miles as it foamed over boulders, rippled over rocks or glided calm and peaceful in a majestic reach. At Aberedw the Edw poured in its waters through a rocky, tree-lined gorge. Behind, on the steep slope of Llandeilo Hill, a series of stratified Silurian rocks rose to a height of several hundred feet and extended like gigantic masonry for a mile or more. These were the Aberedw Rocks so beloved of Francis Kilvert. He called this valley 'a dream of intoxicating beauty'. 'Oh Aberedw, Aberedw,' he says in his Diary, 'I never pass by thy enchanted gorge and look up through the magic gateway of thy Rocks, without seeming, for a minute, to be looking in at the gates of Paradise, just left ajar.'

It was in a cave at the foot of these rocks, so tradition says, that Llewelyn, the last Prince of Wales, hid on the night before his death, only to be betrayed by the blacksmith whom he had engaged to put his horse's shoes on back to front to deceive his enemies. He rode to his death at Cilmeri, a few miles beyond Builth Wells.

From the brow beyond Erwood village, the distant Black Mountains came into view; in summer paled to azure; in winter a dazzling rampart above the brown, snowless foot-hills. Where the valley widened at Glasbury and Llowes, lush meadows billowed like the sea as soft breezes swept over them.

We left the valley at Clyro to climb to the Begwn's brow, from where we overlooked the Bachowey valley and Painscastle, with its castle mound, and faced the Radnorshire hills beyond. Seasons were a good month later in these upland districts, enabling us to enjoy the advent of spring and summer first in the lowlands and then in the uplands.

Autumns reached both uplands and lowlands simultaneously, and while valley orchard boughs bent with rosy apples, hillside rowan berries shone in the sun. Boys stuffed their pockets with conkers and chestnuts, and each day autumn hues waxed more splendid on valley sides and bracken slopes.

Nothing could surpass the lovely winter evenings when the moon shed her silver beams on that sylvan river scene, softening the boulders, lighting up the ripples and casting soft shadows of trees on road and river. It paled to silver-green the gentle dips and swells of nearby banks and hollows and clothed the distant slopes in a diaphanous veil of peace and tranquillity.

Full of youthful exuberance, we were amused by very trivial things. There was, on the bus, a day when patriotism ran high and everyone extolled the virtues of his own nation and emblem. Margaret Macormack, standing ready to alight, delivered a parting shot, 'Well, you can sit on a rose, you can sit on a leek, you can sit on a shamrock, but you can't sit on a thistle,' and was unwittingly jolted onto the lap of a policeman on the front seat as the bus pulled up suddenly.

On Mondays we were made to sit three in a seat to make room for adult passengers using the bus to travel to Builth market. Though we complained, we were actually little inconvenienced. We giggled one morning at a passenger's collar-length hair, so peculiar in those days of short back and sides. In the evening we found him at a cottage door, half-way through the badly-needed cut. To our intense amusement he was obliged to board the bus with a close crop on one half of his head while the other half remained untouched. He returned the following day for the job to be completed.

What happy days they were, with plenty of friends to share the fun and excitement. Each day we looked for some new diversion and were rarely disappointed. It was marvellous, of course, when the bus broke down. This happened on several occasions, but always on the homeward journey, though the boys hopefully scattered nails and tacks in its path while waiting each morning. What fun we had! Innocent fun. I'm afraid we were quite oblivious to the noise we made, which must have deafened the driver and any grown-ups aboard.

Although the days were long I cannot recall being tired. Most of us had examination results equal to those of pupils living near the school, and we certainly outdid them in fun and excitement.

All too soon schooldays were over; we had to go our separate ways. A happy chapter in life had closed.

20. Social Life

There was little social life in the country when we were young. Spring and summer provided the pleasure fairs, the anniversaries, the school outing and sports. In autumn and winter we had to make do with harvest festivals and a concert or two.

Concert organisers were careful to fix their events so as to avoid clashing with those of neighbouring parishes, for all depended on the patronage of the same folk. They tried, too, to arrange their entertainment when there was a moon, for then, even if skies were overcast, there was sufficient light to find the way. One or two events, however, were held annually on a fixed date and took no account of the phases of the moon. Then the night could be so pitch black that a lantern was essential.

For young children a pitch black journey added a spice of fear to the excitement. Walking within the lantern's pool of light, our hands clasped tightly by those of our parents, we felt cosily secure. Giant, long-legged shadows climbing the hedgebanks were pleasantly alarming: who could say what ogres lurked in the darkness. Early evening seemed like the depth of night. We seemed to be going from nowhere to nowhere, with no beginning and no end—the circle of light a kind of treadmill, keeping us constantly in the same place. The sudden heavy breathing of a cow behind the hedge startled us. Here and there a solitary, feeble light from a distant farmhouse window pierced the darkness. In the intense stillness we caught the voices of fellow-travellers. A moment's pause soon resolved their identities and we travelled on together, the extra number providing an added sense of security.

Whatever the weather, all able-bodied folk turned out for a local concert, for should one be missed there could be a long wait for the next. If the night was wet, people dressed accordingly, removing their protective garments before reaching the light of the concert room, to arrive looking their best.

With beaming faces they entered the room, scanning the assembled audience, acknowledging first one then another. All were bubbling with high spirits, anticipating the rare luxury of an evening's entertainment in a warm room amongst rows of friends. The room buzzed with chatter till the chairman mounted the platform; then everyone settled back comfortably in his seat, prepared to listen with rapt attention to every item. Most regular artists were *eisteddfod* competitors, so the standard of performance was, on the whole, quite good. All items were vigorously encored, not only in appreciation but to prolong the entertainment; even then the end came all too soon. Groups travelled home together till their roads diverged, each family travelling the final stretch alone.

Each year Christmas Eve brought the annual *eisteddfod,* or concert, at Painscastle. During the day the trap was washed, its cushions brushed and its lamps cleaned and replenished with candles for the journey.

When we were infants a night ride was a novel experience. Nestling together in the darkness under the cosy rug, between our parents, we felt snugly secure. The trap lights sapped the colour from the verges and made the hedges on either side look ghostly and unreal. They picked out the pony's moving flanks and caught the limpid eyes of sheep and cattle in gateways. The clip-clop of the pony's hoofs and the low rumble of the solid tyres sounded loud in the stillness. It seemed like witching-time. Perhaps witches, with their green-eyed cats, were sailing overhead on their broomsticks: perhaps mischievious will-o-the-wisps, with their treacherous lights, hovered over marshes, luring people to their deaths in some boggy morass. Several people had seen their weird blue lights in the bog, below Cae-blaidd, by the Milw brook. It was pleasantly frightening to think of them from the safety of our parents' protection. The tortured call of a screech-owl came out of the blackness to chill our spines. A rabbit screamed a cry of despair to the unheeding darkness. We could not guess our whereabouts, for all the familiar landmarks were blotted out.

At Rhos-goch shop a soft light shone from Tom and Nancy's window by the roadside. As we pictured them sitting by their cosy fireside our dark trap-ride suddenly seemed less attractive. We forded the Bachowey brook as it hurried through the darkness to the mill race, our lamps picking out the foot-bridge on the left. The familiar, dull rumble of the millstones had ceased and the old mill was strangely silent.

At Painscastle we stabled our pony at Pendre Farm and groped our way along the lane to the lighted windows of the hall, meeting others converging on the same place. After our dark ride even the soft light of the hall dazzled our eyes as we settled down on the narrow, wooden seats, insensible to their discomfort, to listen avidly to the evening's long programme. Before the end our eyes were heavy with sleep. On the homeward journey the dull rumble of the wheels and the rhythmic trot of the pony lulled us to sleep. Back in the fold Mother's voice roused us to consciousness. We were lifted down in a drowsy stupor and stumbled our sleepy way to bed.

Apart from these annual events there was little entertainment for families. Summer evenings were spent working till bedtime, while distance, weather conditions and the darkness of winter kept most folks by their firesides. The waggoner spent much of his time in the stable, where the horses' bodies exuded heat: for there was no cosier place on a winter's night. The stable lantern, suspended from a beam, shed a cosy glow on the dusty, cobwebbed stone walls. A rich smell of hay emanated from the sloping hayracks above the smooth-worn, polished mangers, to mingle with the acrid smell of the stable floor. The waggoner took great pride in his horses, grooming them till their flanks shone, his every job accompanied by the slow crunching of oats, hay and chaff.

Those men thirsty for beer had to face a five or six mile round trip, for our village, as far back as I can remember, boasted no pub. On one or two evenings a week, when work was done, young men from the farms congregated in the village. They had no clubroom, but met in a shed at the Royal Oak, once the village pub but now a shop, to chat and play a game of quoits. The shed offered no seats and only a candle for light. Nevertheless they enjoyed their get-togethers and any passer-by might have heard their roars of laughter.

Dad served on one or two committees and was occasionally called upon to preside over a concert or a local *eisteddfod.* We were always pleased to see him dressing up to leave—being waited on hand and foot by Mother—knowing that discipline would be relaxed in his absence and Mother would tolerate a few noisy games.

Country women had very little social life or, for that matter, leisure time of any sort, their work keeping them busy from morning to night. Their only regular outings were to church or chapel on Sunday and to town on Market day. Mother's interest lay in her poultry and her family and she appeared well content. Like many a country housewife she had an

Newchurch, showing Church and rear of Rectory.

Royal Oak, Newchurch: post office and shop.

unsophisticated, innocent mind, neither knowing, nor wishing to know the seamy side of life. There were no daily newspapers to carry news of city crimes and vice. Country folk enjoyed their own weekly local papers, with news of places and people they knew. Here, where everyone knew everyone else, people guarded their characters jealously and took care to do nothing they'd be ashamed for others to hear about.

The year we arrived at our new farm the whole countryside had been shaken to its foundations by the Armstrong murder case in the local town of Hay. We children, of course, knew nothing of this, for such subjects were never discussed in our hearing. However, many years later, when the topic came up, Dad surprised us by saying he had travelled by rail from Hereford to Whitney-on-Wye, our nearest station, a couple of days before the event, in the company of the solicitor, Oswald Martin, to whom Armstrong, after having poisoned his own wife, had handed a poisoned scone, begging him to 'excuse fingers'.

Except for one or two who had been away in service, most housewives spent their lives in the same district, never straying farther afield than the local market towns. Before her marriage Mother had worked for the Cory family, the Cardiff shipowners, but even so probably saw little of city life. After leaving their service she never again came face to face with Mrs Cory, but they corresponded every Christmas for over fifty years until Mrs Cory's death at a ripe old age.

Mother with the Cory children.

In those days it was unheard of for a decent woman to smoke or enter a public house. Anyone who did so was labelled 'no better than she should be'. This disgust for drink was passed on to us; we would have nothing to do with a young man whose breath smelt of liquor. Those who enjoyed the occasional glass took the precaution to carry small black sweets called Nippits, to disguise the smell.

Our parents, being Chapel-goers, disapproved of whist drives and dances, but one year the school managers, of which Dad was Chairman, voted to hold a whist drive and dance instead of the usual concert to raise funds for the school outing. It was the first event of the kind that our parents had ever attended and Mother was appalled to see husbands and wives dancing with partners other than their own spouses. 'That sort of thing is all right for the young folk,' she maintained, 'but for married folk I call it disgusting.' Playing cards, too, met with her disapproval—these she labelled 'the devil's playthings' and argued that they encouraged cheating and gambling.

In our mid-teens our eagerness to attend dances met with stubborn opposition. We overcame the problem by inviting a couple of my school-mates for weekends when dances were due, making it difficult for our parents to refuse permission for us to attend. And in those days dressing for a dance was almost as exciting as the dance itself, especially when there were several of us together, showing off and admiring each other's outfits.

I well remember my first evening dress, ordered from a mailing firm. When it arrived I could hardly wait to get the parcel open. It was a pretty, sky-blue taffeta, with box-pleated frills and cap sleeves. I was thrilled with it, but Mother, fingering the material, said, 'Well, I don't know what sort of material this is, it feels like paper. I'm afraid it won't wash. No, I think it'll have to go back.' I felt near to tears at the thought of losing it. As luck would have it, before Mother's mind was finally made up, a friend called Maggie arrived on the scene. At the first opportunity I took her aside, briefed her on the story and begged her support. When Mother produced the dress for her inspection and voiced her doubts Maggie who, like us, had never before seen taffeta, fingered the material in a knowledgeable way and said, quite convincingly, 'Oh, yes, I would say that that will wash quite well.' So the dress was kept, and luckily it did wash well. But no one thought of ironing problems and the first touch of a hot iron took a piece out of a sleeve. This time my precious dress was saved by Mother's clever needle.

Occasionally our evenings were spent entertaining or visiting friends. One place we particularly enjoyed visiting was Gilfach-yr-hoel Farm,

Author (left) and Mu outside Penwain.

where we often spent an enjoyable evening listening to gramophone records, interspersed with plenty of fun and laughter. Like Francis Kilvert before us, 'we crossed the silver Milw below Penvain by the plank bridge, where the brook was still running clear over its green tresses and under its fringe of trees. Then up the beautiful mountain side among the golden gorse and rusting fern.'

Once, as we rounded the wainhouse corner where Kilvert was shocked to find the daughters of the clergyman who then farmed there 'assisting at the castration of lambs', we were embarrassed to come upon a dog and bitch engaged in procreative activity. Mr Beavan, the farmer, emerging from the wainhouse, put his foot behind them, saying, 'Come out, old dogs, amalgamating about the place!'

The place was exactly as Kilvert had known it and the hospitality still as ready. Miss Beavan's first words, following her greeting, were invariably the same: 'Put the kettle on, Edith,' and we were soon sitting down to tea in the cheerful, sunny kitchen, before making a semi-circle around the fire to listen to Harry Lauder on the old gramophone, which often had to be wound up halfway through the record.

We would, of course, have welcomed more social activities but their very infrequency made them the more enjoyable. We found almost as much pleasure in the anticipation of events as in the realization of them. Then, every moment was savoured to the full, every ounce of enjoyment wrung out, and the happy hours stored away to be relished over and over again in retrospect.

Towards the close of a summer's day, when evening's peace was on the meadows and the music of the brook clear in the stillness, I loved to steal away and wander within the confines of the farm, alone with my thoughts and daydreams. Lost in thought, fleeting glimpses, as of a previous existence, occasionally flashed across the edge of my consciousness, only to disappear, like a dream upon waking, before they could be grasped. Nothing could be more relaxing than a pastoral stroll, hemmed about by the soothing evening sounds: the far-off bleating of a sheep; a distant lowing cow; the coo of a cushat; the drowsy content of birds settling down for the night in the safe concealment of full-leaved trees. At dusk the ghost moth hovered over the hedges and owls flew past on silent wings. A different light or atmosphere constantly changed familiar scenes, so that they never palled. Such scenes become indelibly stamped upon the memory, to be recalled when birds are silent and trees bare; they become our 'roses in December', a hearth of warm memories for the days when youth has fled.

Edith and Miss Beavan, Gilfach-yr-hoel.

21. The Market Bus

By slow degrees motor transport came to our district in the late 1920s, to change and ultimately transform our lives. Each new vehicle was at first a nine days' wonder, but soon became commonplace and taken for granted. A bright yellow lorry replaced the corn-merchant's old covered waggon, completing the journey in a fraction of the time. When the first baker's van arrived it was welcomed with open arms, for besides bringing us wonderful white bread, it closed the baking ovens for good and ended the gorse-tushing and upheaval of baking day. The grocer's van saved housewives the drudge of carting heavy grocery items from market and gave them a more leisurely market-day.

One by one young men became the proud owners of motor-cycles, bursting with pride as they opened the throttles to attract everyone's attention. With a girl-friend on the pillion-seat they sped away to distant places which till now had been well out of reach. In the silence a motor-cycle could be heard approaching miles away. The sound of one in the distance sent us scampering down to the lane gate to see who was passing, confident that it would be someone we knew who would pull up for a chat. Not to be outdone, one local middle-aged man purchased a machine, but being less venturesome than the younger men he took no chances on sharp corners, always dismounting to make sure nothing was approaching before venturing to ride round.

Over the years a car or two put in an appearance. These were solidly built vehicles that stood plenty of wear and tear. Once acquired they were kept for years on end, their registration numbers known to all for miles around. After a few elementary instructions the drivers learned by trial and error; there were no driving-tests.

It was the market-bus that brought most benefit and pleasure, especially to small-holders and cottagers who had previously been obliged to walk to town on market days. Those with traps used them less and less until they were finally relegated to some dusty shed, there, with shafts aloft, to end their days.

The bus ride itself was no match for an open-air trap ride on a fine day. It was the company that everyone so enjoyed. Market journeys were jolly, social occasions, rather like day-trips, with friendly, animated country folk laughing and joking and calling to each other across the bus. Everyone was welcomed aboard with nods and smiles of greeting and a quip or two from the wits. The drivers were cheerful, willing chaps, ready to carry messages or undertake shopping orders for all and sundry.

Farmers' wives came laden with baskets of poultry, butter and eggs. One particularly inquisitive old dame always wanted to know, of those around her, 'What 'ave you got taking today?' On the return journey she quizzed people on what they had made on their produce. Folks tried to ignore her but she persisted till she got an answer. But when she grilled her neighbour on how much he made on his turkeys at Christmas he said he didn't know. 'Aye but you *do* knah,' she insisted. 'Well I sha' tell ya then,' was his brusque reply.

On the return journey, baskets laden with provisions were stacked aboard, everyone lending a hand. News gathered during the day was shared and lively animated talk echoed around. The eyes of the market-piert were a touch brighter than normal, their loosened tongues additionally entertaining. All passengers alighted to goodbyes, good wishes and jocular advice on how to conduct themselves in the coming days.

In later years city folk on holiday in the district were fascinated by the market journeys. They were mystified when, for no apparent reason, the driver pulled up at a field gate, until they heard him remark, after several minutes, 'No sign o' Mrs Jones yet, but she'll be 'ere in a minute, sure to.' As she was spotted running and panting with her heavy baskets some might jocularly shout, 'Come on, Mrs Jones, pierten-up or it'll be time to come back afore we gets there.' Climbing aboard she might say, ''Ow long you bin waitin', Jack? Our clock was stood and I didna know no aim what the time was.' Such a remark would invite a bit of leg-pulling from the men on board and some spirited rejoinders from Mrs. Jones. There would probably be further waits at gates or road-junctions, to make sure no one was left behind. Perhaps some one would be waiting to hand the driver a shopping-list, with the request, 'Please to bring these few things for me, Jack,' sure of a willing response. To city folk it all seemed so friendly and matey and, though unfamiliar with the local parlance, they loved the fun and repartee, and many were forced to revise their previous concept of the countryside as a dull and lonely place in which to live.

* * * *

By the time we had reached our mid-teens there was an annual pre-Christmas shopping trip to Hereford, twenty-five miles distant. The thought of such a trip sent our spirits soaring as we visualised the festive decorations, the lighted shops heaving with exciting gifts, the jostling

Author (front) in late teens.

crowds and the pleasure of the journey. As there was no pub in our village, several men took advantage of the trip to spend a few hours at the shrine of Bacchus while the rest of us did the round of the shops.

Eagerly we feasted our eyes on windows glittering with tinsel, displaying a rich variety of tempting gifts that made us long for deeper purses. We shopped mainly at Marks and Spencer, where an excellent selection of useful presents was on display for not more than five shillings each. Still less expensive but quite acceptable gifts could be purchased at Woolworths, where nothing was priced above sixpence. There was little difficulty in finding suitable gifts and little danger of buying something a person already had, for people's possessions were few and known to everyone.

The precious hours passed all too quickly; too soon we found ourselves boarding the coach, with bulging bags and empty purses, albeit well satisfied with our purchases. Everyone looked forward to an entertaining journey when the revellers, with tongues well-oiled, tore themselves away from the taverns and staggered, bleary-eyed to the coach. One, in particular, could be guaranteed to provide amusement and wit as, unsteady and talkative, he took his place on the front seat. Immediately the coach started up he proceeded to light his pipe. Match after match was struck, but either the match burned his fingers as he paused to voice some witticism or he failed to focus on the pipe, with the same result. By the time we reached home the floor around him was strewn with dead matches, the pipe still unlit and the air bristling with expletives. As the journey neared its end the thought of the hostile reception he could expect from his wife sobered him up somewhat. Anxiously he wiped the steam from the windows to try to assess his whereabouts. Finding nothing but fog and darkness he grumpily muttered, 'Gor! ya might as well look for Jerusalem!'

22. Retrospect

The world of my childhood still had about it something of the stability and permanence of previous generations, when people spent a lifetime in the same district and nothing seemed to alter. With enormous advances in science and technology my generation has seen more changes, barely noticed at the time, than all the previous ones put together. Only in looking back to my childhood years do I realize the transformation that has taken place.

My native heath has been radically reshaped, to the extent that it no longer resembles the territory I once knew. The narrow leafy lanes have been widened to accommodate modern traffic; the high wayside hedges replaced here and there with wire fences that cry out for some greenery to hide their nakedness. Pretty corners have been sacrificed for vision and speed. Thanks to road widening and chemical sprays, fields and hedge-banks, once ablaze with flowers, have now put on a sober hue. Friendly wooden gates, on which young folk sat to chat and old men leaned to ponder, have disappeared, and with them the craftsmen who made them. In their place stand ugly, clanging gates of steel, unfriendly and uninviting. Footpaths, no longer used, are overgrown and lost. At road junctions signposts direct tourists through this once inviolate territory. On every farm huge new barns, raw and incongruous, dwarf the old stone barns of yesteryear. The market bus, once welcomed so warmly, has outlived its purpose and is no more.

Newchurch School, long since redundant, was awakened for a few short weeks to portray Clyro School in a recent television series based on Kilvert's Diary, before returning again to the arms of Morpheus. The village chapel, so full of memories of people and happenings, has yielded its front lawn to the road wideners, and like the little church finds its Sunday seats mainly empty. The smithy is no more, the anvil silent. There is nothing to show where the wheelwright plied his trade.

Gone too are the old folk, many with toil-bent frames and furrowed faces, whose distinctive characters had been shaped by hours of solitude and meditation. Their places have been taken by a generation fashioned by today's media into a more universal mould. The old dialect, once heard on all sides, is remembered only by older folk; it is neither used nor understood by the young.

Materially, of course, people are far better off, though possibly less content. But few, I imagine, would chose to return to the sweat and toil of pre-war years. Nevertheless we fondly remember that simple, uncomplicated world and the homely folk who peopled it. Those days and scenes are gone forever; they live only in our memory.

Mother in her late 60's.

Glossary of Dialect and Unfamiliar Words and Phrases

A

'anna 'alf raddled their chops: *plastered lipstick on thickly*
anunt: *opposite*
any eft o' people: *a huge crowd*
a purpose journey: *journey for a specific purpose*

B

beetle: *large wooden mallet for knocking in stakes when hedging*
boont: *butt with the head*
boosey: *cattle manger*
boughten: *bought, not home-made*
bracking: *cracking of egg-shells by young birds prior to hatching*
bree: *on the bree—stampeding in fright from the gadfly*
brought up on a mud floor: *came from humble stock*
brown-sheelers: *ripe brown nuts*
bulleyheads: *small fish*
butted: *topped and butted turnips—topped and tailed*

C

chats: *dry dead sticks for kindling*
clet: *piece of cast-iron shaped to fit inside a smoothing iron*
clooking: *Clucking*
conjurer: *a person who works charms*
cootch: *covered store of root-crops*
cootched up: *nestled up*
cratch: *rack or pen (sheep cratches)*
cushat: *dove*
cutting: *touching, moving, affecting*

D

dout: *blow out (candle or lamp)*
drawts: *spring-balance*

E

elder: *udder*

F

fairing: *gift of money to spend at a pleasure fair*
fountain: *large cast-iron kettle with tap*
fullish: *foolish*

G
giving tongue: *whining (of foxhounds) as they picked up the scent*
goose-cub: *goose-coop*
gull(ies): *goslings*

H
hacker: *short-handled bladed instrument used for hedging*
hetherings: *long twigs used for binding and neatening a hedge*
hile: *to attack with horns*
hugger-mugger: *in a muddle*

I
I be up to yet: *I am, so far*
I da' knah no aim: *I have no idea*
I warn there was a good dell there: *I suppose there was a large crowd there*

L
leathern bats: *so called because of their leather-like wings*

M
market-piert: *merry after a few drinks*
meowkin: *scarecrow*
mixen: *dung-hill*
morning wood: *wood dried overnight for kindling*
muck: *manure*
mundle: *wooden stirring implement*
munt: *mountain pony*
mye: *tread down hay*

O
ognel: *contrary, unco-operative*
oona: *won't (will not)*
oont: *mole*
oonti-tump: *mole-hill*

P
peewits: *lapwings*
pierten up: *liven up*
pikle: *pitch-fork*
(to) pill: *feed with oatmeal pellets*
pitch: *incline, hill*
pooty: *pretty*
pooty 'igh in the breast-bon (bone): *conceited, proud*
puck: *picked*
pugging: *getting the comb caught in tangled hair*

Q
quist: *wood pigeon*

R
rising the ashes: *clearing the fallen ashes from the ash pan*
roadsters: *men of no fixed abode who travelled from place to place seeking work*

S
sheelers: *hazel nuts*
silly ahld cooten: *silly old fool*
sooble: *agitate*
spreeding muck: *spreading manure*
squoze: *squeezed*
squat up: *wedge up (wheel)*
stanked up: *dammed up*
steen: *large glazed earthenware vessel*
stock: *peck*
stripped: *milked*
stuck up: *conceited*
sway: *hinged cast-iron arm to pull forward over the fire, for suspension of cooking-vessels*

T
three o'clock yesterday evenin': *three o'clock yesterday afternoon (In Radnorshire the word afternoon was never used by the locals. The period between dinner and tea was evening; any time after tea was night.)*
thrahin' on it in some form: *exerting all his strength*
tiddling: *an orphan lamb fed on cow's milk*
tollant: *hay loft*
trow: *trough*
tump: *hillock*
tush: *drag*
tushed bundles: *dragged bunches of long sticks*

U
up in 'er sittin's: *sitting up in bed after an illness*

W
wainhouse: *shed for gambo and waggon*
warn: *warrant, suppose*
whimberry: *bilberry*
will make the back on you: *will benefit you greatly*

Y
yender: *yonder*
yorks: *leather strap worn below knee over trousers*